WELCOME TO
YOUTHSEARCH!

If you have limited time to prepare to lead your YouthSearch group, look at QUICKSCAN™ on page 3. You will find enough basic information in QUICKSCAN™ to help you get started.

YOUTHSEARCH offers you an opportunity to work closely with other people and to learn about topics that are crucial concerns of everyday life. YOUTHSEARCH is designed

✓ to help you prepare to lead a group;

✓ to give you plenty of practical ideas and options;

✓ to be faith-oriented and biblically based;

✓ to help you build rapport so that group members are willing to share honestly their concerns, questions, and insights;

✓ to be easy to use.

You may have decided to form a small group because you and people you know are concerned about a particular subject. We hope that by completing the sessions in this book, you will

✓ learn ways of inviting people into your group and of making them feel welcome;

✓ gain insight into yourself, your life, and the lives of the youth in your group;

✓ understand how the Bible and Christian faith apply to issues affecting you and the other members of your group;

✓ see other ways for people to work together in small groups.

We believe that YOUTHSEARCH will help youth and adults to struggle together with questions about how to live faithfully. As the members of the group begin to work together, they will

✓ offer one another support and encouragement as they grow in faith and become the people God wants them to be;

STRESS & TIME

✓ listen to one another actively and effectively to become aware of what is most important in their lives.

The secret energy of YOUTHSEARCH is in your group. Every group is a unique combination of personalities and abilities. This book is simply a tool to guide and support the members of your group as they learn and grow together in faith.

Regardless of the order in which you use them, the books in the YOUTHSEARCH series build on one another. Each book will introduce skills that you can use in future small-group study.

If you are the leader of a YouthSearch group, please read the articles in the back of this book. They will answer some of your questions and will help you prepare to lead the group. If you are a participant, you may want to read the leader's articles in order to learn ways of helping the leader and of developing rapport among members of the group.

We want to share your excitement about using YOUTHSEARCH. We also want to hear about your concerns. If you have any questions about YOUTHSEARCH, feel free to call Curric-U-Phone at 1-800-251-8591 and to ask for the editor of YOUTHSEARCH.

Have a terrific time with your YouthSearch group!

Your editorial team for this volume of YOUTHSEARCH:

Debra G. Ball-Kilbourne
editor

Gail G. Bock
assistant editor

Branson L. Thurston
coordinating editor

QuickScan™

For an overview of each session, use QuickScan™.

ICONS
The icons in each session suggest activities. The icons in YouthSearch are explained on page 4.

MARGINAL NOTES
The notes in the margins include ideas and instructions for activities, as well as questions for discussion.

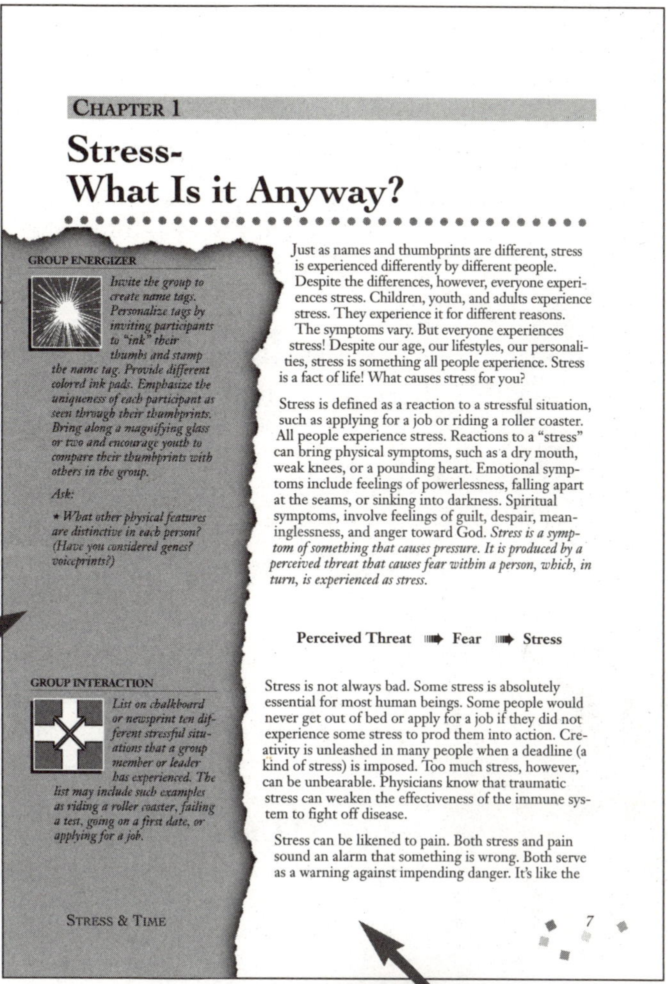

MAIN TEXT
Each member of the group should read or at least look through the main text, the content of the session.

Chapter 1
Stress— What Is it Anyway?

GROUP ENERGIZER

Invite the group to create name tags. Personalize tags by inviting participants to "ink" their thumbs and stamp the name tag. Provide different colored ink pads. Emphasize the uniqueness of each participant as seen through their thumbprints. Bring along a magnifying glass or two and encourage youth to compare their thumbprints with others in the group.

Ask:

• What other physical features are distinctive in each person? (Have you considered genes? voiceprints?)

GROUP INTERACTION

List on chalkboard or newsprint ten different stressful situations that a group member or leader has experienced. The list may include such examples as riding a roller coaster, failing a test, going on a first date, or applying for a job.

Just as names and thumbprints are different, stress is experienced differently by different people. Despite the differences, however, everyone experiences stress. Children, youth, and adults experience stress. They experience it for different reasons. The symptoms vary. But everyone experiences stress! Despite our age, our lifestyles, our personalities, stress is something all people experience. Stress is a fact of life! What causes stress for you?

Stress is defined as a reaction to a stressful situation, such as applying for a job or riding a roller coaster. All people experience stress. Reactions to a "stress" can bring physical symptoms, such as a dry mouth, weak knees, or a pounding heart. Emotional symptoms include feelings of powerlessness, falling apart at the seams, or sinking into darkness. Spiritual symptoms, involve feelings of guilt, despair, meaninglessness, and anger toward God. *Stress is a symptom of something that causes pressure. It is produced by a perceived threat that causes fear within a person, which, in turn, is experienced as stress.*

Perceived Threat  Fear  Stress

Stress is not always bad. Some stress is absolutely essential for most human beings. Some people would never get out of bed or apply for a job if they did not experience some stress to prod them into action. Creativity is unleashed in many people when a deadline (a kind of stress) is imposed. Too much stress, however, can be unbearable. Physicians know that traumatic stress can weaken the effectiveness of the immune system to fight off disease.

Stress can be likened to pain. Both stress and pain sound an alarm that something is wrong. Both serve as a warning against impending danger. It's like the

Stress & Time

7

For more help preparing to lead a YouthSearch group, read "Welcome to YouthSearch!" beginning on page 1, and the articles in the back of the book.

Stress & Time

3

ICONS

Icons are pictures or symbols that will show you, at a glance, what to do in each part of the session. These are the icons used in YOUTHSEARCH:

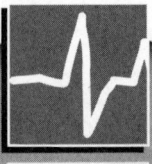
PULSE POINT indicates a time to assess the group's feelings and to find out what's been happening in the participants' lives since their last meeting.

GROUP ENERGIZER refers to an activity that focuses the group's attention on the topic. The energizer may be an icebreaker at the beginning of the session or an activity during the session that gets the group excited about the topic.

WORSHIP means a time of prayer, music, guided meditation, or celebration.

DISCUSSION asks you to engage members of the group in discussion by asking questions such as those listed in the marginal notes.

GROUP INTERACTION indicates an activity such as a role-play, simulation, or small group discussion that involves members of the group in learning together.

BIBLE STUDY asks you to invite the group to explore a Bible passage.

REFLECTION indicates a time of quiet reflection on an issue or a question.

DECISION POINT alerts you to consider a decision about 1) including new members in the life of the group, 2) dividing the chapters so that they can be used for more than one period of time, 3) extending a chapter beyond one session because of the group's interests or concerns.

BEFORE NEXT TIME identifies what leaders and/or participants will need to prepare for the next session.

YOUTHSEARCH

INTRODUCTION

"If it is difficult to define and measure stress, it is even more difficult to calculate its cost. It costs . . . in terms of . . . human misery." (From *The Complete Guide to Stress Management*, by Chandra Patel; Plenum Press, 1991, page 4.)

Stress exists! Everyone experiences stress. forty-three percent of all adults suffer adverse health effects from stress. 70 to 90 percent of all physician office visits are for stress-related ailments and complaints. (From *The Stress Solution*, copyright © 1993 by Lyle H. Miller, Ph.D., Alma Dell Smith, Ph.D., and Larry Rothstein, Ed.D. Reprinted by permission of Pocket Books, a division of Simon & Schuster, Inc.)

Stress can turn a clear face to one filled with "zits", seemingly overnight. Spirit-breaking stress can be linked to school absenteeism and the rising numbers of teen suicide attempts. Although statistics exist, no one needs to plow through a list of them to affirm that teens experience the effects of stress on physical, mental, and spiritual health . . . as do children . . . as do adults. Stress is more than an isolated incident; it is the product of an escalating, cultural lifestyle.

A brief look at the "self-help" books available in bookstores convinced me that glib prescriptions for relaxation, setting priorities, making lists, and the like provide—at best—superficial solutions to a cultural dilemma. They are superficial because stress is caused by something far more fundamentally wrong than the challenge to "juggle" the demands of exhausting lifestyles. **Many of us have made a god of activity**. We need to learn how to **be** not how to **do**.

That challenge is one I lived with in writing this volume of YOUTHSEARCH.

As I began writing this, I came to at least one conclusion. The seeds for change do not, necessarily, lie within our own culture and world-view. In most civilizations, there come moments when it is helpful to step outside one's own period and place, discovering what solutions others have found. Today, this is already occurring as interest grows in Native American spirituality, Eastern religions, or New Age teachings. These may bring fresh perspectives. But are those perspectives consistent with larger beliefs in our Judeo-Christian heritage?

How refreshing to discover, within our own Old Testament tradition, a heritage that is both consistent with our Christian faith and helpful in reducing our distress. The Hebrews began as nomads, adapted to life among the Canaanites as farmers, and about 400 BC, developed writings now known as the Wisdom tradition. These writings include the books of Job, Proverbs, Ecclesiastes, three books in the Apocrypha, plus many psalms.

I have found in these Old Testament writings, with its concept of *shalom* (peace) and *Sabbath* (rest), an alternative to modern stressful living. I am convinced that the loss of Sabbath time, which has occurred largely within the past generation, contributes in a major way to modern stress and the breakdown of family and community structures.

According to Israel's Wisdom writers, a fundamental order lay hidden within the universe that applied to both nature and humans. Persons could reflect upon nature and the animals and draw conclusions from parallels. The wise observed life and attempted to live in harmony with this rhythm and order. The result was joy, well-being, wholeness, security (*shalom*). Refusal to do so resulted in chaos (stress).

Book learning did not necessarily lead to wisdom, but rather careful observation of human experience and common sense was required. God willed that life be orderly and stable and that honesty, justice, and faithfulness prevail. "The fear of the Lord is the beginning of wisdom, and the knowledge of the Holy One is insight."(Proverbs 9:10) "If any of you is lacking in wisdom, ask God, who gives to all generously and ungrudgingly, and it will be given you." (James 1:5)

Thus we cannot manage either time or stress. **God manages all!** We can observe God's order and choose to accept or reject it. Those who choose to live in harmony with God will be wise; those who do not are foolish.

I am realistic enough to know that picking up a philosophy from a distant time and place, and dropping it into our 20th century time slot, will not result in automatic transformation. In a pluralistic culture such as ours, we cannot force Sabbath rest upon everyone. We can, however, evaluate basic principles from the Wisdom tradition, adapt them to our own setting, and begin to model *shalom* lives within our communities.

Alternatives to our frazzled, anxious way of life do exist. Some of those alternatives are suggested within the pages of this book. Stress and burnout need not be the order of the day. Play, beauty, peace, and joy are gifts from God to those who live in harmony with God's laws and created order.

Shalom, my friends!
Nancy Regensburger

Nancy Regensburger has worked as both a Christian educator, and district project manager in The United Methodist Church. She holds a Masters of Theological Studies from a Roman Catholic Seminary and is trained as a spiritual director in that tradition. Nancy writes curriculum for United Methodist, Roman Catholic, and Presbyterian publishers. She is the mother of two grown sons and lives with her husband in Vassar, Michigan. Nancy loves to walk, enjoy quiet moments, and laugh!

Chapter 1

Stress— What Is it Anyway?

GROUP ENERGIZER

Invite the group to create name tags. Personalize tags by inviting participants to "ink" their thumbs and stamp the name tag. Provide different colored ink pads. Emphasize the uniqueness of each participant as seen through their thumbprints. Bring along a magnifying glass or two and encourage youth to compare their thumbprints with others in the group.

Ask:

★ *What other physical features are distinctive in each person? (Have you considered genes? voiceprints?)*

GROUP INTERACTION

List on chalkboard or newsprint ten different stressful situations that a group member or leader has experienced. The list may include such examples as riding a roller coaster, failing a test, going on a first date, or applying for a job.

Just as names and thumbprints are different, stress is experienced differently by different people. Despite the differences, however, everyone experiences stress. Children, youth, and adults experience stress. They experience it for different reasons. The symptoms vary. But everyone experiences stress! Despite our age, our lifestyles, our personalities, stress is something all people experience. Stress is a fact of life! What causes stress for you?

Stress is defined as a reaction to a stressful situation, such as applying for a job or riding a roller coaster. All people experience stress. Reactions to a "stress" can bring physical symptoms, such as a dry mouth, weak knees, or a pounding heart. Emotional symptoms include feelings of powerlessness, falling apart at the seams, or sinking into darkness. Spiritual symptoms, involve feelings of guilt, despair, meaninglessness, and anger toward God. *Stress is a symptom of something that causes pressure. It is produced by a perceived threat that causes fear within a person, which, in turn, is experienced as stress.*

Perceived Threat ⇒ Fear ⇒ Stress

Stress is not always bad. Some stress is absolutely essential for most human beings. Some people would never get out of bed or apply for a job if they did not experience some stress to prod them into action. Creativity is unleashed in many people when a deadline (a kind of stress) is imposed. Too much stress, however, can be unbearable. Physicians know that traumatic stress can weaken the effectiveness of the immune system to fight off disease.

Stress can be likened to pain. Both stress and pain sound an alarm that something is wrong. Both serve as a warning against impending danger. It's like the

STRESS & TIME

DISCUSSION

Say:

"Everyone responds to stressful situations differently. A specific event may cause you great stress, but may not bother me at all."

Invite the group to review their list of stressful situations.

Ask:

★ *Are all ten of the stressful situations stressful for everyone in our group?*

Select an individual who reacted strongly to a specific situation and another who reacted only mildly to the same event. Invite them to discuss why the same situation causes two different reactions.

body sends up a red flag, "Hey, stop and pay attention to me!" Stress and pain allow a species to detect threats and react to them. Without this sensitivity, no species would survive.

It's how we handle stress that can cause problems. This depends upon individual differences. The emotional responses of some people aren't easily triggered and don't stay on the alert very long. Others perceive real or imagined danger around every corner. Some feel challenged by danger, rallied into action. Others shrink from it and become immobilized. A roller coaster ride can be great fun for one and a terror to another. Neither approach is right or wrong—just different!

We all experience stress in certain situations. My son, David, tried skydiving during his college years. He knew better than to tell me ahead of time. When I heard the news, my heart did flip-flops! However, when David was in high school, he was stressed-out by the prospect of making a short presentation in speech class. All his alarm systems went on alert! One person's nightmare can be another's stimulation.

It's important to pinpoint our areas of stress and the underlying fears and dangers. When we identify the fear, we may discover it's mushroomed out of proportion. Think, for example, about when you were a child and afraid to go to bed at night. Perhaps you were like many other little children, sure that there was a monster under your bed. How did you react? Were there real monsters? Of course not! But, thinking that there were monsters was enough to make you afraid. Today, you are probably not afraid that you are in grave danger each time you walk by your bed! Your fears from childhood, at least this one, have probably ended. What finally convinced you that there were no monsters? (One child who was afraid that lions lived under his bed dismissed his fears when his father told him that "all the lions went South for the winter." By spring, he had completely forgotten about his fear. While new "monsters" were a part of his life as he grew older, such as asking for a date and trying out for the soccer team, this particular fear never returned.)

Sometimes thoughts, rather than actual events, create stress in our lives. When we encounter the perceived

REFLECTION

Encourage members of the group to reflect on their "monsters," or fears.

Ask:

★ *What are your monsters? friends? peer pressure? school? work? parents?*

DISCUSSION

It is not vital for members of the group to discuss their responses to the chart of perceived threats and fears. However, if time permits and you wish to include a discussion time regarding the chart, share your list first. Modeling is important, particularly when risk is involved. Model your ability to risk important information about yourself before inviting or expecting youth to do the same

DECISION POINT

If you are studying this material over two sessions, break here. Close by reminding participants that despite our differences, we are loved by the same God. Read aloud Psalm 139:1-18.

Begin your next session with "How Do I Respond to Stress?" Use the Group Interaction found on page 10.

STRESS & TIME

---

threat—the monsters— head on, we may discover they are only "paper tigers." When we unmask what makes us feel as we do, we can make decisions about whether to walk through, sidestep, or change the situation. We can make decisions to say "Yes" or "No." We may not be able to remove the perceived threat, but we can choose our response.

ASSESSING MY STRESS

Circle the situations in the chart that frighten you. Add to the list any additional situations that frighten you.

Perceived Threat	Fear
Dentist	Physical pain
Final exam	Failure
Bungee jump	Pain/death
Secrets about my family	Social rejection
Not getting into college	Failure
Car accident	Disability/death
Poor health	Pain
Arguments	Conflict/violence
Wearing the wrong clothes	Social rejection
Physical punishment	Pain/humiliation
Marriage	Commitment
Nuclear war	Death
Asking for a date	Social rejection
Additional threats:	Additional fears:

HOW DO I RESPOND TO STRESS?

Psychologists tell us that by nature (genes) and nurture (training) we develop widely different personalities. For example, the same loud noise that frightens one child may intrigue another. Some people react fearfully in almost any situation while others remain happy-go-lucky, no matter what. While the division is an oversimplification, psychologists divide us into two trait/temperament types:

Inhibited	Uninhibited
Anxious	Bold
Serious	Happy-go-lucky
Cautious	Carefree

Likes the familiar　　Likes new situations
Careful　　　　　　　Takes risks
Defensive　　　　　　Aggressive
Reactive　　　　　　　Proactive

Place a dot along the continuum below at the point you think is closest to your trait/temperament type. Do you tend to be more inhibited? uninhibited? Perhaps you are a combination of both. Many people are!

Inhibited   **Uninhibited**

There are negatives and positives for both types. Obviously uninhibited persons may experience less observable stress. They may die young, but they're having a blast in the meantime! Uninhibited folks express fewer complaints, enjoy life to the fullest and are fun to be around.

On the other side, inhibited persons, who feel greater sensitivity to danger, appear to show more sensitivity toward the feelings of others, nature, and beauty. Their deep feelings extend from fear to love. Many great musicians, authors, and artists, are inhibited by nature, even withdrawn. The uninhibited, however, may behave like something of a clod when it comes to interpersonal relationships. They just come blastin' on through!

It's not that being one way or another is right or wrong. Healthy teens can be either inhibited or uninhibited. Most are a combination! If we know ourselves, however, we can handle stress in the way that is best for us. Plus we can make intentional changes in our approach. Knowing ourselves is the first step in transforming stress from a minus to a plus.

HOW CAN I KNOW MYSELF?

Read Psalm 139:1-18

God created each person and knows more about us than our very best friend. God knows us even better than we know ourselves. In spite of all our faults

---

GROUP INTERACTION

Provide markers, fingerpaints, and paper. Invite group members to use supplies provided to color a shape, symbolizing their individual personalities. Use intense or calm colors, primary or subtle ones, colors around the edge, through the middle, and so forth. Again, you should model the ability to risk discussing personal information. To do so, show your own symbol to the group. Then, encourage group members to choose a partner. Invite the partners to explain symbolic self-portraits to one another. As group members share self portraits with a partner, they may check whether the self portrait matches the way the partner perceives the situation. One way to check out perceptions is for each partner to ask the other, "Is this the way you see me? If not, do you see me as more or less inhibited?"

BIBLE STUDY

You may want the group to read Psalm 139 from different translations of Scripture. Read them aloud, so that the full meaning of the verses sink in.

BIBLE STUDY

Ask:
* Who knows you better than anyone else?

* Do you believe God knows you better than that person does? If yes, talk about your answer.

* Does it help you to accept yourself when you know God knows all about you and still loves you?

* Do you believe it helps to overcome fears and stress if you pray to God about them? why or why not?

and hang-ups, God loves and accepts us. We are loved, not because of things we do, how we look, or what we own. God loves us because we are God's creation.

> Search me, O God, and know my heart;
>   test me and know my thoughts.
> See if there is any wicked way in me,
>   and lead me in the way everlasting.
>   (Psalm 139:23-24)

Notice that in these last two verses from Psalm 139, the writer prays to God to look deep into his or her innermost part and remove the hurtful (wicked) ways that may be present. This is scary business! Each of us has hidden away many secrets.

The psalmist is not fearful, however, of God's scrutiny. He or she knows God will continue to love him or her no matter what. The psalmist asks God to guide us in ways that ultimately lead to everlasting life. This means the way of God chosen by his faithful ancestors.

The closer we come to God, the nearer we come to the real us, the ones created in God's image (Genesis 1:27). God can help us learn to know ourselves. Just ask!

WE'RE NOT STUCK!

Modern psychologists and the Bible agree on this. If we are born and nurtured to a certain personality disposition, we are not stuck in that slot forever. Humans are more than the sum total of their biology and environment. Behavior is not fixed or rigidly predictable. Scientists say something in the brain circuit is responsible for the fact that we can start something and then stop. A dieter reaches for the sack of candy and then pushes it away. We sometimes attribute such an action to willpower. Willpower enables us to control our behavior, to turn from a fearful response ("They'll make fun of me if *I just say no*) and choose a good and responsible action ("No, thanks.").

The Bible calls this victory over sin. We do not need to stay stuck in our fears and failures. We can walk straight through our stress and pain. Now to him who

DISCUSSION

Ask:

★ Where (how) do you find shalom (peace) in your own life?

★ How does it help overcome chaos?

GROUP INTERACTION

Encourage group members to privately review the list of dangers and fears they circled on the chart in an earlier part of this session. Ask them to write at least one threat they identified on a slip of paper. Collect these. Respecting anonymity, record threats on newsprint or chalkboard.

Ask:

★ Which of the suggestions identified on page 12 and 13 and marked by a bullet • might be helpful in dealing with each particular threat?

---

by the power at work within us is able to accomplish abundantly far more than all we can ask or imagine. (Ephesians 3:20) Believers are not powerless people because they can tap into the power of God.

FROM STRESS TO SHALOM

The people of Israel who wrote the Old Testament over 2,000 years ago lived with stress too. However, they worked out a lot of good ideas about how to find the opposite of stress (chaos) which they called shalom. In the Scriptures the Hebrew word *shalom* usually translates into English as *peace* or *life*. The concept signifies more than the absence of conflict or death. Shalom is a peace that comes when everyone in the whole group experiences joy, security, wholeness. Shalom means living life here and now to its fullest. It's not a dull passive peace, but a peace of beauty, sensitivity, wholeness. Those who achieved it are characterized as happy or blessed.

Old Testament people believed that humans are largely responsible for their own destiny. They believed that life held tremendous opportunities if one would seize them. Options exist. In every situation, humans can make a wise or foolish choice. The wise person and the fool are the two opposites in Wisdom literature.

This literature taught that a fundamental order lay within oneself and extended outward to the whole universe. When individuals lived in harmony with that order, they moved from chaos to shalom. The wisdom for finding this peace came from God.

HINTS FOR REDUCING STRESS

These ideas may help you live in harmony with your true self—not your egotistical, materialistic, shallow self—but the loving self created in God's image.

• **Avoid situations you know will prove too stressful.** Forget about going out for the school musical if you know performing before an audience makes you up-tight. If you really don't enjoy the track team, quit!

• **Manage it.** Keep the pressure under control by eating right, getting plenty of sleep, and exercise.

REFLECTION

Can you come up with additional stress reducing suggestions? Will it help you live in harmony with your true (best) self, the self God wants you to be?

WORSHIP

Read Psalm 32:1-7 aloud.

Begin prayer by inviting youth to close their eyes and become very quiet. Say: "Take God on a tour of your heart. Describe to God all the feelings hidden there—joy, pain, anger, fear. These emotions belong to you and you need not be ashamed of them. Welcome them and allow them to either stay or to pass. Talk with God about your feelings and try to listen."

Pause for a moment.
Close with the Lord's Prayer.

BEFORE NEXT TIME

Photocopy Psalm 32:6-7 or print the passage on several index cards. Distribute one card or photocopy to each group member. Encourage the youth to put the passage near their beds and use it as a reminder to pray throughout the week.

STRESS & TIME

However, some situations ought never be accepted. For example, physical abuse should never be tolerated by anyone. Ask for help from a trusted adult and get out of the situation immediately!

• **Know your abilities and interests, shortcomings and limitations, and live within them.** Learn to say no when asked to do something that does not interest you or fit with your talents. Say no when you're already too busy. Delegate work to others when possible. Don't decorate the whole gym for the prom by yourself.

• **Be kind to yourself.** Don't set impossibly high goals and standards. Don't require perfectionism; settle for the best you can do in each situation. Forgive yourself when you do fail. Take time out for fun.

• **Turn your liabilities into positive assets.** A shy person is often a good listener. Focusing on listening ability can remove pressure and open doors for friendships. For example, a loud aggressive teen may cause tension because he can get on other's nerves, but those qualities can make a top football player.

• **Pray about it.** Pray about your dangers, fears, stresses. It feels good to unload on someone. God can keep a secret. Sometimes we think we should pray only high and holy thoughts. But God wants to hear everything going on in our lives—even our feelings of sadness, doubt, anger, despair. (Check out the psalmist's feelings in Psalm 139:19-22.)Every night before you sleep this coming week, center in on your own deeper self and tell God exactly how you feel. Look back over the day and talk with God about the times of upset and times of peace.

Use this passage to remind you to pray to God.

> Therefore let all who are faithful
> offer prayer to you;
> at a time of distress, the rush of
> mighty waters
> shall not reach them.
> You are a hiding place for me;
> you preserve me from trouble;
> you surround me with glad cries
> of deliverance. (Psalm 32:6-7)

CHAPTER 2
Returning Home

PULSE POINT

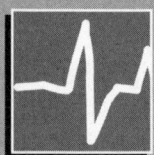

Ask the group to think about these questions:

★ *Did you tell God about your feelings this week?*

★ *At the end of each day, were you able to identify times of peace or upset and talk with God about them?*

GROUP ENERGIZER

Large groups may want to form smaller discussion groups during the "energizer." Choose one of the following suggestions and:

Say: *"As a group, talk about your favorite spot in nature. It might be a vacation site, a scene of unusual beauty or a small secret spot near your home. How does being present in this spot affect your burn-out level?"*
OR
Say: *"As a group, talk about an outdoor activity you enjoy. How does it affect your feelings of stress?"*

The earth is the Lord's and all that is in it, the world, and those who live in it. (Psalm 24:1)

We are earthlings in the true sense of the word, creatures taken from the earth. Scholars tell us that in Hebrew the word for Adam, *adamah*, is not a proper name, but the word for earth. God created this first creature from the dust of the ground and breathed into him the breath of life (Genesis 2:7). "You are dust, and to dust you shall return" (Genesis 3:19b) The earth is truly our home.

Earth is star dust coalesced into a rocky ball, shaped and given purpose by God's creative love. The earth sustains bacteria, insects, food plants, flowers, and other flora and fauna. All human cells, bones, brains and consciousness are crafted from the raw materials of the earth. Our blood contains properties of sea water. We depend upon the earth for life in the form of food, water, and oxygen. Earth is a beautiful pulsating entity, of which humans exist as an integral part. We participate in its harmony.

The call to be in harmony with the earth is strong in younger children. They love to jump in mud puddles, make angels in the snow, run through downpours with rain streaming down their cheeks, and dig in sandboxes. As we grow older, a sense of separation sets in. More and more time is spent in houses, in cars, and in school. Toys and trinkets, theme parks and video games, TV and movies, money and success take over. Forgotten is the fun of rolling in grass, scratching in dirt, climbing trees, running with the wind. Lost is the sense of mystery, wonder, and gratitude.

Each of us looks for a home in the deepest psychological and spiritual sense. We need to belong; and when we experience separation from nature, we may ache with loneliness or be beset with anxiety.

If we know who we are, why we are, and where we

DISCUSSION

If your group is fairly large, you may want to form smaller discussion groups.

Say: *"Talk about an outdoor activity you enjoyed as a child. Do you still feel connected to nature? when? how?"*

Ask:

★ *Do you agree that our society's attitude toward our environment is one of use and control rather than respect and gratitude?*

Explain.

★ *What are some results of our culture's being out of touch with God's creation?*

★ *Think of human effects on air, water, land, and animals. Do you think this alienation may cause us stress? Why or why not?*

GROUP INTERACTION

Invite group members to go outdoors and pick up an item from nature. Provide containers for any who choose dirt or water.

When the group reassembles, invite everyone to meditate upon their object.

Then say:

"Try an experiment. Find something from nature—a rock, a leaf, a shell. Feast your eyes upon the object. Look at its parts. Observe the whole. Gently caress it with your fingers. How does it feel? Smell it. Does it have a distinct aroma? Can you describe its smell?"

STRESS & TIME

---

belong, then the normal tensions and pressures of our days are easier to bear. A sense of *shalom* prevails. Alienation from nature, from self, and from others often go hand in hand. When we fear nature's forces, we may distrust our own bodies and feelings, and respond with hostility toward the stranger.

The earth and other creatures provide what we most need—love, mystery, wonder, hope. If we are to be healed of the fears and stresses of modern living, we must seek interludes of intimate contact with nature. It is our home. We are a part of nature. The natural world is where we belong.

AWAKENING OUR SENSES

We can rediscover our sensual qualities by reconnecting with nature. We can add richness to our lives by allowing ourselves to feel more deeply. This can be practiced but requires that we relax, slow down, touch, and listen.

The world of nature surrounds us. We do not need to travel to a windswept island or deep forest, nor do we need to make a retreat to a monastery or camp (although all these are great). We live surrounded by the earth and its fruits. Even those who live in an inner-city still walk on earth, bathe in flowing water, feel the rush of wind, hug a tree, watch a pigeon or spider, caress a stone or piece of wood. Further, bricks are made from clay, taxicabs from steel (iron alloyed with other metals) rubber tires are made from rubber trees, fuel is made from dead plants and animals hundreds of millions of years old. In urban areas, earth has been recycled by humans. Urban settings provide as much material for reconnecting with nature as do rural settings, if we look for the source and relationship of things.

CONNECTING WITH OTHER CREATURES

The creeping things of the earth will give you lessons,
and the fish of the sea provide you an explanation:
there is not one such creature but will know
that the hand of God has arranged things like this!
In his hand is the soul of every living thing
and the breath of every human being.
(Job 12:9-10 New Jerusalem Bible)

15

Discuss the following questions:

★ *How did you feel about your object?*

★ *What did you learn?*

★ *Is your object dead or alive? Explain.*

★ *If "recycled by humans," what was its source in the earth? (Use a dictionary if necessary.)*

★ *Did this sensing of an object from the earth help you feel more relaxed, peaceful?*

★ *If so, how and when might you do similar sensing experiences in the future?*

DISCUSSION

Identify an animal (fish, insect, bird) with whom you have (had) a friendship. What good qualities does the animal have? What lessons can the animal teach you now?

Do you think a relationship with an animal can reduce your stress level? How might that work? How can you connect more often with other creatures?

GROUP INTERACTION

Have the group decide if they want to do one of these stress reducers together. If so, do it together.

Psychologists today tell us that pets are more and more becoming primary relationships. Blood pressures actually drop as we stroke a dog or a cat. Autistic children appear able to relate to dolphins, and elderly folks in nursing homes can be made joyful by the visit of a mutt from the dog pound. Chimpanzees are serving as limbs for quadriplegics, and dogs assist in finding missing earthquake victims. Children are not alone in their love of Garfield, Bambi, or Snoopy. Youth and adults love them too. Animal friends can soothe away tensions and fears.

Not everyone has a pet. Even those who do not have a pet may be close to an animal. For example, a youth group from an urban, Midwestern city pooled their resources and adopted a dolphin through a marine ecological society. They receive regular updates on how the society is working to reduce the slaughter of dolphins by large fishing and canning operations. Caring, in this way, for a creature of God's hand allowed land bound youth to have a vitally important harmonious, primary relationship.

The abuse and killing (to extinction) of animals, fish, birds, and insects in our time is symptomatic of our stressed relationship with God's creation. When the environment and creatures cry out in fear and pain, it affects humans at the deepest level of their being. There is then no *shalom* in the creation, including within ourselves.

HELPFUL HINTS FOR REDUCING STRESS

• **Find a "home" in nature.** Search for a place that seems sacred to you and return to it often. Spend time there alone. Read, write in your journal, or just relax.

• **Walk in the rain.** Get soaked to the skin and enjoy the cleansing healing of water. Play in the snow. Build a snowman or a snow fort, make snow angels, sled.

• **Get in touch with the earth by gardening.** Don't wear gloves. There are few things more satisfying, both emotionally and spiritually than the feel of earth in our hands. When raising flowers or vegetables, you participate in nature's cycle of birth, life, death, rebirth. Even in the midst of an inner city you can garden in a pot, a box, or another small container. It's not the size of the garden that is important!

• **Visit a farm.** Walk through corn fields, feed a farm animal, ride a horse, milk a cow.

• **Take a day each month and serve nature.** Pick up litter, help with a recycling program, assist with environmental education at a nature center, lobby for environmental causes, volunteer to walk or feed animals, contribute food or money to your local humane society.

• **Befriend an animal and share your secrets with it.** If you do not have a pet, go animal watching. Find a secluded area in nature, away from human activity, and sit, listen, and watch. Animals, birds and bugs will soon appear. Take some binoculars for close-ups. Or take a drawing pad.

• **Feel the buoyancy of water by swimming, the power of waves by surfing.** Or get in a canoe or flat-bottom rowboat, slip into a shallow secluded area and silently watch the plants, animals, insects and birds.

• **For a nighttime prayer experience, (provided that you live where you can safely do so) slip away to a hidden spot, lie flat upon the ground and gaze up at the stars.** Enjoy a friendly visit with the God of the universe.

DECISION POINT

This is a good breaking point, if you are using this material over two sessions. If you are closing your session invite group members to write reflections on their journal page. Begin your next session by praying: Speak to us, O God, as we seek to live in greater harmony with you and all creation. Amen.

THE VOICE FROM THE WHIRLWIND

The Old Testament book of Job is a literary masterpiece. Its poetry is breathtakingly beautiful. The unknown author of Job was probably an Israelite living around the fifth century BC but with knowledge of literature of other countries, particularly Egypt.

The popular point of view at that time was that bad people suffer and good people prosper. God willed it that way and God's justice saw to it that things happened in that manner. Thus a person who suffered pain and stress must have committed terrible sins. There was no other explanation offered at the time Job was written.

The book of Job challenges this theory with the story of a rich, happy, righteous man who suffered immensely. His cattle were murdered by enemies and his sheep burned in a fire, his sons and daughters were killed when the house in which they were eating collapsed in a hurricane. Job himself got ulcers from his head to his toes. His wife turned against him and suggested he curse God and die. Everything that could go wrong, did.

Job's three "good" friends argued that his sins had caused his sufferings. Repentance would change his bad fortune. Job insisted that he had committed no sins. His tortured soul cried out to God for an answer. His pain was all encompassing. Job's stress was physical, psychological, and spiritual.

The book consists mainly of Job's arguments with his friends. In his final speech, however, Job challenges God directly (chapters 29-31) and God answers through a fierce storm (chapters 38-41). The meaning of God's words are not easy to discern, and scholars disagree about the meaning. Let us attempt to see whether God's response to Job's stress might provide us with some clues to our own stresses.

BIBLE STUDY

The following is an outline of Job 29–42.

Job's final defense of himself and challenge to God

- Chapter 29—Former happiness
- Chapter 30—Present misery
- Chapter 31—Defense of Job's own righteousness

Job's young friend gets angry

- Chapter 32-37—Elihu lectures Job for insisting he is righteous, and putting God in the wrong

God's voice through the whirlwind

- Chapter 38—Nature
- Chapter 39—Creatures
- Chapter 40—Evil and wickedness (the beast and sea monster may be symbols)

Close

- Chapter 42—Epilogue
- Chapter 42:1-6—Job's final answer to God
- Chapter 42:7-9—God criticizes Job's friends and favors Job
- Chapter 42:10-17—God restores Job's fortune

Ask youth to silently read Chapter 30.

Say:

"Describe Job's areas of stress in your own words. Are these stressers from which we suffer today?"

Read aloud Job 30:26. Invite group members to tell about a time when they 'looked for good and evil came, waited for light but darkness came.' Now check verse 28a. Invite youth to

The book of Job narrates the story of a man's extreme stress, his challenge to God, and God's answer to him. The reader is left to figure out the meaning. Put a plus in front of every statement that you think fits with the meaning and minus in front of those that do not.

_____ God's reply does not fit with Job's problem. It doesn't make sense.

_____ God cares for creation and its creatures. We will find peace when we do the same.

_____ God is the source of all wisdom.

_____ We belong to God. We have no control over God nor should we make demands.

_____ There is no answer. It only tells us that God's care continues when everything goes wrong.

_____ The appropriate response to the wonder and beauty of creation is humility.

_____ Circumstances changed from bad to good when Job's attitude changed.

_____ Faith must remain even when understanding fails. Even though angry, Job still believed in God.

_____ Life is a mystery and we will never know why fear and stress happens to us.

_____ The story of Job is not just about a man who lived long ago and far away but about every human.

What additional ideas can you offer to explain the meaning of God's voice from the whirlwind? Record them below.

STRESS & TIME

describe a time when they had to 'go about in a sunless gloom.'

Now have the youth form two groups—one to report on Chapter 38 and one on Chapter 39.

Ask:

★ *What do you think is the message in God's word, from the storm?*

Finally, read Chapter 42:1-6 together. Answer the plus and minus statements found on page 19. Discuss the answers as a group.

WORSHIP

Read the biblical text and writer's commentary. Invite members of the group to pray in silence.

Encourage youth to reflect on how Job's experience with stress can help them in everyday life. Ask them to write these reflections on page 21.

BEFORE NEXT TIME

Ask the group to read Proverbs 10— 29, practical sayings about life from a wise old person to a youth.

FROM DESPAIR TO HOPE

For I know that my Redeemer (Defender) lives,
and that at the last he will stand upon the earth;
and after my skin has been thus destroyed,
then in my flesh I shall see God,
whom I shall see on my side,
and my eyes shall behold, and not another.
(Job 19:25-27)

Job has sought, but not found, someone from among kin to stand by his side. His intimate friends abhor him and those with whom he lives turn against him (Job 19:19). His flesh is rotting and his bones cling to his skin (19:20). He believes that God is the cause of his misery (19:22). Yet in the midst of abandonment, in a stunning display of faith, Job loudly asserts (23-24) that in the end time, after his flesh is destroyed, God will defend him as a friend. Not everything will get straightened out in this lifetime. Job glimpses a widened vision of God's justice as one that extends beyond the grave.

In quiet, ask God to show you one way that Job's experience with stress can help you in your everyday life. Write your ideas in your journal.

Journal Page

Chapter 3

Pressure from Others

GROUP ENERGIZER

This activity will help youth learn more about themselves and serve as a community builder. Bring enough apples for each participant. Each participant may choose an apple and tell why it is like himself or herself. Enjoy a snack!

PULSE POINT

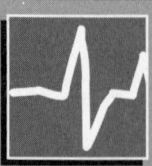

Ask: What sayings in Proverbs 10-29 might prove helpful to you everyday? for your group? for your family?

REFLECTION

Say: "Use page 28 to Write about a time when you felt forced outside a circle. Write about how it felt. How did it turn out? What adult could you turn to for support if you were in big trouble?"

The book of Proverbs contains advice from a wise teacher given to a young man. For this session you were asked to read Proverbs 10—29.

This session will explore the stress in relating to others, including family members. Look up Proverbs 11:29a, 14:1, 14:26, 17:6, 17:25, 20:7, 23:22-27.

Would any of the biblical advice be helpful for your own family? Jot down below particular advice that could help your family.

OUR NEED TO BELONG

The threat of being forced outside the circle of acceptance looms as one of our most stressful fears. We need others in order to survive. A child needs its family. Teens crave approval from peers. Couples consummate their deepest love in marriage. People form towns and cities for mutual support. We worship in faith communities in order to stand together before God. Nations form around a common life and for mutual defense. We need connection with others whom we value and who love us. Alienation from others is scary!

GROUP INTERACTION

Have group members identify categories of relationships (parents, employers, teachers) that cause stress in everyday life. List these on newsprint or chalkboard.

Ask:

★ What is a primary cause of stress in each of these relationships?

★ What might be the underlying danger or threat?

Form smaller groups and suggest that each smaller group choose a conflict situation from relationships you listed and role play it in front of the group. Then as a total group work to identify danger, threat, and fear each specific form of stress takes.

Ask:

★ How might we resolve this situation peacefully?

BIBLE STUDY

Invite group members to read Psalm 128 in unison with volunteers reading the running commentary (found on page 23) after each verse.

Abandonment by family, peers, and community presents a threat that causes stress, often at a subconscious level. If our relationships are based upon our "delivering the goods" to satisfy the demands of others, then we will always fear not measuring up. Human relationships remain shaky at best. Friends are not always faithful. A good friend who moves away or turns against us, the breakup of a dating relationship, or the death of a family member, can cause crippling pain. The fear of such pain may even cause us to withhold our love. Sometimes, picturing our pain in symbols or words helps us deal with that pain. In the space below write the words that capture some of the pain you have felt in relating to friends, family members, team mates, teachers and others.

MOVING FROM STRESS TO SHALOM

Read Psalm 128.

1 Happy is everyone who fears the
      Lord,
   who walks in his ways.
2 You shall eat the fruit of the
      labor of your hands;
   you shall be happy, and it
      shall go well with you.
3 Your wife will be like a fruitful
      vine
   within your house;
   your children will be like olive
      shoots
   around your table.
4 Thus shall the man be blessed
   who fears the LORD.

5 The Lord bless you from Zion.
  May you see the prosperity of
    Jerusalem all the days of your life.
6 May you see your children's
    children.
  Peace be upon Israel!

RUNNING COMMENTARY OF PSALM 128

1 The main point of the psalm is made at the very beginning. The one who obeys the commands of God will be blessed. Those who recognize God as Lord and are humble before God will want to be obedient to God's laws. God's commands are found within the Scriptures, and for the psalmist, they would be primarily the Ten Commandments.

Sometimes we imagine we can live as we please, breaking whatever rules we wish. When distress and disorder result, we blame others and God. However, we have no one to blame but ourselves when the natural consequences of disobedience to the moral order bring chaos and threaten to wreck our lives.

The psalmist holds that the acceptance of God as the foundation of our lives results in true peace. Happiness, then, is a blessing from God, not something we achieve ourselves.

2 A right relationship with God results in right relationships with other people. In our everyday lives we will find this happiness. Work or school, whatever we do daily, will go well. Prosperity follows. Our work will provide for our needs. Thus in the most routine parts of our lives, which we often take for granted, we experience God's blessings.

3-4 If we obey God's commands we will be happy in the families with whom we live each day. We sometimes wish we could escape our families but our writer disagrees. He draws two images to symbolize his own family relationships. His wife resembles a fruitful vine, probably a grape vine, because she produces children and other blessings.

His children are like shoots sprouting from the roots of an olive tree. Our psalmist probably chose this image because of the value of the olive tree—it provides fruit, wood, olive oil and medicines. An olive tree lives for hundreds of years. Even today,

BIBLE STUDY

Ask:

★ *Do you think living in obedience to God's word would eliminate stress? Explain. (See Psalm 119:1-3, 9-11, 47-48)*

★ *What rewards do you want from your future work?*

★ *Do you think there is a connection between stress in our homes, school, nation, and world?*

★ *Is there shalom at each level?*

DECISION POINT

If you are using the material in this chapter over more than one session, end here. Pray for group members. Encourage members to pray for persons from whom they feel alienated.

PULSE POINT

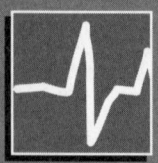

If you are beginning a new session, spend time sharing reactions of group members to the study materials or their involvement to the group.

YOUTHSEARCH

GROUP ENERGIZER

Distribute telephone wire (available at most craft stores). Make symbols of group members' involvement with the group. Invite each member to share his or her symbol.

REFLECTION

Provide your group members with a period of quiet during which each member can reflect on the following questions:

★ *Is your home usually characterized by shalom or chaos? A little of both, perhaps?*

Remind group members that journal pages are a private matter. They can write openly. What they write will not be shared during the course of a group meeting.

---

the olive branch symbolizes peace. In Israel, both the vine and olive tree were regarded as blessings bestowed upon humans by God. The psalmist tells us that his family gives him great joy.

5 The writer moves beyond the joys of individual relationships to the nation. Jerusalem, both the religious center and political capital of the country, is envisioned as peaceful and prosperous. All bodes well for a nation when people find joy in their work and their families. Peace begins at home.

6 In Israel a long life was regarded as a special gift from God. Those who obey God's commands live in health, harmony and prosperity and a long life will result. "May Shalom be with Israel," is the closing blessing. All's right with the world.

GRANDMA IS A SUNFLOWER!

The poet in Psalm 128 wrote in picturesque language. He imaged his wife as a fruitful vine and his children as olive shoots around his table. These images evoke in us an understanding of his family that narrative might not convey. Pictures sometimes pop into our minds without a mental connection. But if we reflect, there is usually a common quality between the images and that which it symbolizes.

On your journal page, write in a vertical column down the left side, the names of all persons who live in your home. After each, write the name of a plant which reminds you of that person. The first thing that pops into your mind is probably the best. Why did you choose the particular images to represent the persons who live in your home? What does this exercise tell you about the level of stress in your family?

All families experience some conflict. Read God's laws as given in the Ten Commandments, Exodus 20:1-17. When stress dominates your family, are any of God's laws being ignored or disobeyed?

What can you do to help your family become more of a *shalom* family?

Stress between parents and teens is inevitable. Your parents love you, and since your birth have maintained control. All parents must slowly let go. Most fear losing their children. On the other side, kids

STRESS & TIME

GROUP ENERGIZER

Provide art supplies. Invite youth to choose one family member mentioned in their journal reflection and symbolize that individual as a piece of fruit. Ask for volunteers who are willing to share with the group to do so—but respect privacy.

GROUP INTERACTION

Plan a group activity in which youth help others. Examples: work at a soup kitchen, visit a nursing home, hospital, or church members, get involved in a community cleanup project or work camp. Explore summer work camp and mission project possibilities. Carry out your plans, even if that requires doing so after this study has ended.

DISCUSSION

Ask:

★ *Which suggestion is most helpful in dealing with a stressful relationship in your life now? Explain.*

---

are sometimes too eager to break away, wanting freedom they may not be mature enough to handle. Try to appreciate how your parents feel. Ask yourself, "How would I react if I had a daughter (son) like me?" The tug between parent and child is normal and healthy—but also stressful!

Another common area of stress may exist between you and your friends. Competition can cause tensions. Often no one feels genuinely pretty or macho. Others always wear the right clothes, date the neatest girls, make the cheerleading squad. Comparisons are made and we find ourselves lacking. So we try to cover up by not being real. We are unfaithful to our inner self. "Coveting," that is wishing we had what others possess, causes tension (Exodus 20:17). Instead we can identify our strengths, celebrate individuality, rest secure in God's love as we are here and now.

BLESSED ARE THE COMPASSIONATE

Happy are those who are
concerned for the poor;
the Lord will help them when
they are in trouble.
The Lord will protect them and
preserve their lives;
he will make them happy in the land.
(Psalm 41:1-2, Good News Bible)

Relating to people who are less fortunate is one way to overcome stress, grief, and pain within ourselves. Those who set their own problems aside to help others will truly find themselves blessed.

HINTS FOR REDUCING STRESS

• **Extroverts get energy from other people and introverts get it from solitude.** Take time to renew yourself in whatever way fits your personality. If you feel frazzled, pass up the party and stay home with a good book.

• **Be ready to apologize and forgive.** Don't always try to get even. Carrying around grudges and nasty feelings drains your energy. It hurts you more than the other. Clear the air and let go of hurts.

YOUTHSEARCH

- **When communicating with others, chalk off "you" and talk in "I" language.** Don't say, "You always make us late," but rather, "I feel embarrassed when we arrive late." "You" language places blame and makes others defensive. "I" language expresses your own honest feelings and no one can argue with that!

- **Talk over serious stresses with a trusted adult such as a relative, school counselor, social worker, minister.** Talk over problems with God through prayer.

- **Walk through legitimate pain.** When we see pain from a death or separation from a loved one, for example, our natural tendency is to repress it, turn aside, run away. Sometimes we must just grit our teeth, take one step at a time, and walk straight through the pain. Allow tears to flow so healing can begin. Our Christian faith teaches that darkness is followed by light, death by resurrection. Note that we are referring to legitimate pain that is a normal part of all relationships. Pain caused through physical or verbal abuse, injustice, oppression ought not be tolerated. Talk with a responsible adult and get out of the situation immediately!

- **Choose friends who are upbeat, accepting, noncompetitive, and real.** Hopefully these can be found in your church. There is no place for put-downs, gossips, or fakes among Christian friends.

- **Keep life balanced.** From time to time everyone lacks balance. However, exercise, rest, eating healthily, relationships, service, fellowship, and worship work together to keep life from becoming too stressed. Chapter four will focus on the value of balance in our lives.

WORSHIP/CELEBRATION

O Lord, all my longing is known to you;
 my sighing is not hidden from you.
My heart throbs, my strength fails me;
 as for the light of my eyes—it also
  has gone from me.
My friends and companions stand
  aloof from my affliction
  and my neighbors stand far off.
Those who seek my life lay their snares;

GROUP ENERGIZER

Supply construction paper, markers, straight pins and scissors. Instruct youth to create a large piece of fruit to symbolize themselves. Pin the paper fruit on each group member's back. Give each youth a marker. Instruct youth to circulate and as he or she encounters another group member write an affirming statement on the paper fruit of that person.

BIBLE STUDY

*Read the text aloud.
Ask:*

★ *What is the writer's only source of hope?*

STRESS & TIME

WORSHIP

Invite youth to tell about a time they felt everyone had turned against them. Ask:

★ *Do you believe God will continue to love you through the worst of circumstances? How does this make you feel?*

those who seek to hurt me speak of ruin,
and meditate treachery all day long.
Do not forsake me, O Lord;
O my God, do not be far from me;
make haste to help me,
O Lord, my salvation. (Psalms 38:9-12, 21-22)

In the silence tell God about any people in your life who have caused you problems, conflict, fears. Ask God for help in relating to these people.

Pray for special people you love. Does one have a birthday? Is one sick, getting married, or going away? Thank God for those caring folks who are blessings to you. List their names below:

BEFORE NEXT TIME

Every day when you wake up this week, talk with God about at least one special person in your life.

Next time, bring a tape of your favorite music to the group.

Chapter 4

The Rhythm Of Time

PULSE POINT

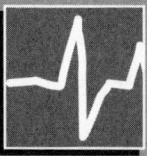

Invite youth to talk about any experiences they may have had of praying for special people last week.

Ask:

★ *Does praying for someone help you relate to him or her better?*

GROUP ENERGIZER

Ask participants to close their eyes. Use a watch with a minute hand. Ask group members to silently raise their hands after a suggested period of time, such as thirty seconds or one minute. No counting aloud of course! Who was most accurate?

Ask:

★ *Was it difficult? easy?*

★ *How do you think our bodies estimate passage of time?*

DISCUSSION

Ask:

★ *How do you explain time?*

★ *Do you believe it is eternal?*

★ *Do you agree with the final paragraph about priorities?*

★ *Do you agree or disagree with this often heard statement: "You're as busy as you want to be."*

WHAT IS TIME?

Time is one of those mysterious things that everyone experiences but few can explain.

Scientists estimate that our earth was formed over 4.6 billion years ago. Approximately 3.6 billion years ago life took shape as a simple cell with no nucleus. Humans arrived about 100,000 years ago. Compared with the existence of the earth, a human lifetime is a drop in the bucket. A mayfly hatches, produces offspring and dies in two minutes. A squirrel lives about eight years. That's a whole lifetime to them. **Time is relative!**

Creation is suspended between time and space. The material world, of which we are a part, travels through time. Time contains no meaning, in and of itself, unless combined with matter. The material world passes away but time is eternal.

Time does not appear to flow evenly. We all know the speed with which time flies when we're having fun and how slowly it passes when we are bored or waiting for something to happen.

We know about time because we are aware of its effects. We see changes in the seasons, the build-up and breakdown of living tissue, the movement from birth to death. While humans do not have an organ for sensing time such as the eye seeing objects, we do possess a time sense. We are able to clock ourselves and be fairly accurate. Our whole physical body is on a clock that moves us through transitions in life, with zits at one stage and gray hair at a later stage.

We have no control over time. It marches forward one hour, one day, one year at a time, and nothing we do can stop it. Our priorities are what make the difference.

STRESS & TIME

BIBLE STUDY

Read aloud Genesis 2:1-3, Exodus 20: 8-11, and Leviticus 25:1-7.

Ask:

★ *What did God do on the seventh day?*

★ *Why is the seventh day holy?*

★ *Do you think God enjoyed creation on that day?*

Explain.

★ *How are humans to observe the Sabbath?*

★ *Who is included in this command?*

★ *In Leviticus 25:1-7, Sabbath rest is extended. What else is included?*

★ *Do you think the idea of Sabbath as a day of rest is a good idea now?*

★ *Why or why not?*

★ *Do you think our society would be less stressed if we observed it? Explain.*

THE SABBATH

Throughout history, religious people have divided time into to two parts: ordinary (profane) time and sacred (holy) time. Ordinary time is the period between any two events. Sacred time represents a remembrance or reenactment of a sacred event that occurred in the past. For example, Sunday morning worship is sacred for most Christians because the first day of the week recalls the resurrection of Jesus. By means of liturgy (rituals) and stories, people pass from ordinary to sacred time and back again into the world. During sacred time people are in deeper communion with creation and the Creator.

For all creation, God blessed the Sabbath as a sacred time of rest. Work alone does not bring human fulfillment. Sabbath puts a brake on our frenzied activity. It provides a rhythm of work and rest, rest and work. That rhythm permeates the whole created order. When we break the rhythm, we experience stress. We feel out of synch, not in the groove. We lose touch with our deepest selves.

Sabbath is a time for the whole creation to stop and enjoy the mystery and beauty of the good world God created. Because that's what God did on the first Sabbath, Sabbath time is holy.

Sacred means to make holy, blessed, set apart as special. Scholars tell us that the root Hebrew word for "holy" is the same as for "healing." The Sabbath provides time for God to heal and make us whole again through rest. Early Christians celebrated both the Jewish Sabbath on Saturday and worshipped together on Sunday because Sunday was the day of Jesus' resurrection. Jesus is viewed as the beginning of a new creation. During his lifetime, Jesus freed the Sabbath from being experienced as a a burdensome obligation to the time of joy God intended.

Sabbath time is more than doing nothing. It is something like what we call "quality time." Some prefer to think of Sabbath not as one special day, but as a quality of life that runs through the other six. The following are words characteristic of the two times.

DISCUSSION

Invite the group to discuss the following questions:

★ Talk about a Sunday when you had a good time.

★ Was it "healing" for you?

★ What are some re-creative activities you do on Sunday that do not cost money?

★ Which is of more value: the time friends and family share with you or money or things they give you?

GROUP INTERACTION

Say: "In small groups, talk about something you created recently."

Then ask:

★ How did you feel about your creation?

★ Afterwards, did you enjoy it or not? If so, in what ways?

★ Have group members affirm each other's creative abilities.

DECISION POINT

Pray and end your session here, if you are using more than one session to explain this material.

Encourage group members to pray for one another in the week ahead.

STRESS & TIME

To Do **(Ordinary)**
Work, school
Exert effort, achieve
Cultivate the earth
Acquire and spend money
Use power
Make a living
Ministry for God

To Be **(Sabbath)**
Rest, reflect, dream
Pray, read Scripture
Enjoy the earth
Share, care for the poor
Creative self-expression
Sense of mystery, awe
Worship God

The people of the Old Testament understood Sabbath time as a little piece of eternity on earth. Since material things will not go with us to heaven, to enjoy **being** rather than **doing** prepares us for our future life with God.

CREATIVITY AS SABBATH TIME

Every human being creates in one way or another. We invent and craft items, using our imaginations and artistic abilities. Think about what you enjoy doing most. That's probably an area in which you are most creative. In the chart below, circle your creative abilities from those listed. Space has been provided for you to add other creative abilities that were not listed. Take a few moments to consider how you are most creative!

Music
Sewing
Giving a Speech
Participating in Sports
Art
Overhauling an Engine
writing
Gardening/Farming
Teaching Others
Scientific Research
Cooking
Debate
Planning Parties and Special Events
Problem Solving
Dancing
Working on a Car
Playing with Children
Acting in a Play
Drafting
Training Animals

31

PULSE POINT

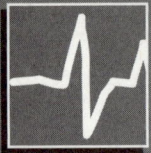

Ask the group:

★ *What activities that you enjoy put stress on our environment?*

★ *How could you change your use of time on Sunday to give rest to the whole creation?*

GROUP ENERGIZER

Provide rhythm instruments: drums, shakers, tambourines, sticks, triangles, and so forth or invite teens to create a rhythm by pounding on a hard surface. Ask for a volunteer to lead and others to repeat the beat.

Ask:

★ *Why is time important to music?*

★ *What would pitch and tone be without it?*

★ *What role does balance play in music?*

★ *How is the beat and silence of music like ordinary time and Sabbath time?*

God made something out of nothing! God is super creative. We use already existing materials. When God finished making the universe, God created a special time, the Sabbath, to rest and reflect in joy upon the creation. Enjoying God's creation, as well as our own, is good use of Sabbath time. Creativity re-energizes our minds and spirits. Our activities on the Sabbath ought not cause stress for the rest of the creation (air, water, earth, animals) because it's their time of rest too.

RHYTHM OF MUSIC

Creation is the language of God. God made the world by calling it into being (Genesis 1). God said, "Let there be" for each element of the created order. The act of bringing the world into being is a continuous process. Every instant is an act of creation. Time moves perpetually forward and creation continues. If we liken God's creation of the universe to the composition of a song, the material world compares to words and time to God's melody. To live in harmony with God's time is like singing a song with God.

Music depends upon harmony, rhythm, balance, and time. There are beats and space between the beats. Without the space, that is, intervals of silence, there could be no rhythm. By varying the timing of notes and rests between, the pitch and tone of an instrument make music.

Music flows. So does time. Our response to music may be a recognition of the inward desire to flow forward in a harmonious manner. We experience such harmony when our thoughts, feelings and actions are dancing to the same beat. Whether it's joy, grief, jealousy, whatever, everything is in synch. Sometimes, however, that does not happen. We feel angry, but we pretend to feel happy, and angry actions get aimed at the wrong person. We feel torn in different directions. Then we experience stress— discord—disharmony. If things get bad enough, we may shut down completely and not permit ourselves to feel anything.

The music we enjoy at a particular time reflects the way we feel within our deepest selves. Something in the music touches where we are. We may say, "This song says it for me." We may prefer smooth harmo-

REFLECTION

Ask group members to play one song, from a favorite tape, to the group. After each song ask:

★ *Do you like the song or not?*

★ *Invite group members to write in their journals how listening to each kind of music makes them feel.*

Ask:

★ *Is it in harmony or discord with your life now?*

★ *Does it seem real or fake?*

DISCUSSION

Ask the group:

★ *Describe a time when you listened to the sound of water, snow, wind, or an animal. Did it relieve tension?*

★ *Would you describe this as Sabbath time? Explain.*

---

nious tones or a wild discordant beat, depending on what's happening in our lives. We like what feels "real." It's always good to feel real, even when those emotions are painful.

A note of caution here. Music reflects our feelings but can also create feelings. Rather than energizing, some music can drag us down. Christians will want to avoid music with constant themes of violence, evil, darkness, death. Such music, while popular in our culture, produces stress, rather than *shalom*.

RHYTHM OF NATURE

For you shall go out in joy,
and be led back in peace;
the mountains and hills
before you
shall burst into song,
and all the trees of the field
shall clap their hands.
(Isaiah 55:12)

The prophet Isaiah described the glorious time when Israel would return from slavery to its homeland. His prophecy used metaphors from creation. He envisioned trees clapping their hands!

There's lots of rhythm and dancing in the natural world around us. Melodies are created by pounding surf, bubbling brooks, swirling snowstorms, hurricane winds, howling wolves, chattering chipmunks. When we join with the balance of action/silence in nature we can experience healing and inner order. When outer harmony touches our inner being, we experience deep peace. Such time can truly become Sabbath time!

RHYTHM WITHIN

The balance of time in God's created order is also present within our own bodies. While being formed in the womb, we listened to the constant beat of our mother's heart. Rhythm is present in the orderly pulsations of our cells and tissues, flow of blood through our veins, biorhythms of our organic systems, the firing of energy within our brains, the racing messages throughout our nervous system.

STRESS & TIME

DISCUSSION

Say:
"Think about your pumping heart and breathing lungs. How do they participate in Sabbath time?"

Perhaps the most obvious action/rest rhythm within is our pumping hearts and breathing lungs.

Most of the time, when we pray, we talk to God. We tell God how we feel, ask for favors, pray for friends. That's appropriate. But if prayer is to be conversation with God, we must also stop and listen. Listening prayer happens when we become silent. Instead of *doing* we are simply *being* in God's presence, open to whatever happens.

A FORM OF LISTENING PRAYER

Centering prayer is a form of a listening prayer. Christians long ago practiced centering prayer. They knew that the experience of being quiet in the presence of God, of halting their busyness and trying to stop thoughts from jumping through their mind was spiritually satisfying. Centuries later, the Quakers and other pietistic movements practiced centering in the presence of God as a primary means of prayer. The Quakers believed that being quiet in the presence of God was necessary if one was to receive "inner light," or spiritual guidance. Today, Christians of all ages and many different denominations practice centering. In a hectic world, centering provides a way of quieting down and allowing us to let go of everything. We want to look deep down inside to the center of ourselves. That is where we can find God. Centering prayer is Sabbath time.

WORSHIP

Invite the group, to participate in a centering prayer experience as you slowly, with long silent periods, read instructions as given . . .

After step 1, "Close your eyes . . ." indicate that anyone not wishing to participate, may simply sit quietly.

Ask:

★ *How was the experience?*

PRACTICE CENTERING PRAYER

• **Close your eyes. Breathe slowly and consciously.**

• **Relax the body,** bit by bit, from the soles of your feet to the top of your head.

• **Feel the support of the chair** and *relax* against that support.

★ What feelings did you have?

★ Were you able to relax? Let go of thinking? Concentrate on your body's rhythm?

★ Did God speak to you? Explain.

★ Might you use this process at home?

BEFORE NEXT TIME

Ask the youth to practice centering prayer. Say: "Write about your reflections in the space provided at the bottom of this page."

• **Pay attention to the rhythm of your own heartbeat or the rhythm of your breathing.**

• **Be aware of God giving you the gift of one more moment of time.** Without the next breath or heartbeat, there would be no more life.

• **Listen for what God may be saying to you through the rhythm of the body God created for you.** Remember that God is present for you now.

At home, it may be helpful to reflect on the important things in your life by writing in your journal pages after you have practiced "centering." The method used for centering is unimportant. **What does matter is that you learn to slow down your thoughts and feelings in order to give attention to God and what God might be saying to you.**

Centering prayer enables the rhythm of your own body to connect with the harmony in creation and in God. The result **is** *shalom*.

STRESS & TIME

CHAPTER 5
Celebration Time

PULSE POINT

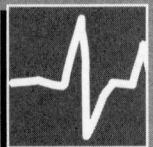

Ask:

★ Did you practice centering prayer at home?

★ Did you prefer to center on your heartbeat or breathing? why?

★ Did it lead you to gratitude for God's gift of time and rhythm?

GROUP ENERGIZER

Ahead of time, place symbols or pictures of holidays such as Christmas ornaments, Halloween candy, a cross, and birthday wrapping paper in a paper bag. Have youth choose one symbol from the bag. Invite group members to make a choice and tell what each enjoys most about the particular holiday they select.

Ask:

★ Is there anything you don't like about a particular holiday?

(Note the examples of distorted celebrations the writer provides.)

STRESS BUSTING CELEBRATIONS

What do birthday parties, Fourth of July parades, spring break, Thanksgiving turkeys, and Holy Communion have in common?

They're all celebrations—and they're all stress busters! Celebrations are energizing time bits that pop up in the midst of routine. These times lift spirits, re-create, give pause for reflection, and are fun. They help us organize feelings, discover meaning, experience *shalom*. Celebrations relieve the tensions of our ordinary lives by affirming times of play and relaxation.

Our modern society so values production, study, work—*doing*—that our well-being, both individually and as a nation, may be in danger. Stress can cause both physical and mental damage, antisocial, and even violent behavior. Further, some celebrations become distorted and bring results that are harmful, not life-giving. Examples of this are serving beer at graduation parties, exploiting sex during spring break, pressuring youth to buy expensive clothes for proms, and hassling Christmas shoppers at the mall. These distortions are misguided quests for happiness. While they may cover pain, they cover joy as well. Celebrations must continually be reevaluated to see whether they remain consistent with the original meaning.

YOUTHSEARCH

BIBLE STUDY

Read Psalm 100. Invite the youth to record words within the psalm that they associate with times of celebration and joy. Invite group members to discuss choices. Note choices on a chalkboard or a large sheet of paper.

Then ask:

★ *What appears to be the purpose of the psalm?*

★ *What reasons are given for praising God?*

DISCUSSION

Have the group think of their Sunday morning worship service. Ask:

★ *What liturgical form invites people to enter into holy time?*

★ *What closes the service and sends people back into ordinary time?*

★ *What sacred event(s) from the past are remembered and/or reenacted?*

STRESS & TIME

MAKE A JOYFUL NOISE

Make a joyful noise to the LORD,
    all the earth.
  Worship the LORD with
    gladness;
  come into his presence with
    singing.

Know that the LORD is God.
  It is he that made us, and we
    are his;
  we are his people, and the
    sheep of his pasture.

Enter his gates with
    thanksgiving,
  and his courts with praise.
  Give thanks to him, bless his
    name.

For the LORD is good;
  his steadfast love endures
    forever,
  and his faithfulness to all
    generations.
                (Psalm 100)

This psalm could appropriately have been used at almost any of Israel's festivals. It may have been sung by pilgrims approaching the gates of the Temple or chanted by a choir within the Temple courts.

HOLY TIME AS CELEBRATION

Holy time is quality time set apart from ordinary time. It contains a God-dimension. It usually remembers or reenacts a sacred event from the past. For example, Christmas is the remembrance of the birth of Jesus. The crèche scene with Mary, Joseph, the baby, and animals is nothing less than a reenactment. A story is told and retold which is not just a story from long ago, but a story that persons now experience as true. As Christians we do not merely celebrate that Jesus came as a baby at some point in history long ago. *We believe that God dwells among us and remains present in the world.*

Religious people pass from ordinary time to holy time and back into the world again by means of ritual (ceremonies) and liturgy (readings and prayers). God invites us to "come apart for awhile."

The Sabbath (Session 4) differs from other religious holidays because the Sabbath was created by God as a special day set apart for *shalom*. Holidays, while still holy time, were established by humans, and usually related to the moon or seasons of the natural world. Time divides into night and day, months, seasons, years. At special intervals, people set time aside to raise their hearts and voices in praise to God. These celebrations became the festivals, holidays, feasts, and pilgrimages of ancient people.

In our own Judeo-Christian tradition, Hebrew people in early Old Testament time, such as Abraham and Sarah, were nomads. They lived in tents and moved frequently, seeking food for their goats and sheep. Since ancient shepherds often traveled by night, they developed a lunar month and calendar. In pagan cultures, worship focused upon the moon and heavenly bodies. A lunar calendar of 29 and 30 days alternately developed very early.

However, after the Hebrew people settled in the land of Canaan (about 1200 BC), they adopted the lifestyle of their farmer neighbors, and their religious festivals became tied to the seasons. They focused on themes of planting, growth, and harvest—the cycles of generation. Good crops literally meant life or death. While the Israelites took over the holidays of their neighbors, they added meaning. The Passover, which was originally a celebration of the barley harvest, received additional meaning as a celebration of the passage from slavery to freedom (death to life) at the time of the Exodus from Egypt. At a Passover supper with his disciples, Jesus associated the bread and blood of the Passover lamb with his own body, about to be broken in death. Centuries of time may change the meaning of liturgical celebrations. But a core base of truth remains.

Most of the worlds religions derived from either nature or revealed religions. Nature religions actually worshipped objects from nature such as the sun, moon, earth, or rain. Our Judeo-Christian ancestors never worshipped creation, only the Creator (See Genesis 1). While we watch the creation to show us truth about God, we also believe God steps into history with special revelations through God's spoken Word in Scripture and through Jesus.

DISCUSSION

Invite the group to think of time as a cycle of seasons. Ask:

★ *What is your favorite season? why?*

★ *Do you think four seasons enrich time, makes it more fun? Explain.*

DECISION POINT

If you are using more than one session to study this material, this is a natural ending place. Pray together: "Thanks, God for the gift of time. Amen."

YOUTHSEARCH

PULSE POINT

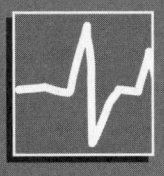

Begin again! What has happened in each group members' life since your last session? Celebrate the good things!

REFLECTION

Have group members select one holiday from the liturgical year and write a story, on page 44, of something good that happened to them during that time. What is the original story of that holiday? Do your stories share in the spirit of the first story?

We might note, however, that times of birth—growth—death—rebirth (resurrection) are primary themes in all religions rooted in worship of (1) the moon, (2) nature, and (3) the life and death of Jesus. Belief in the cycle of life, death, and new life persists as a core truth. It refers not just to resurrection at the end of physical life, but for all the little deaths and rebirths within our lifetime on earth. This hope is good news indeed!

DIVISION OF TIME IN THE CHRISTIAN YEAR

The liturgical year, followed in most Christian churches, conforms to the life of Jesus. The cycle also follows the seasons of the year, and pagan nature celebrations underlie many of our Christian holidays. Notice how the year is balanced by approximately six months of holy time, followed by the same amount of ordinary time.

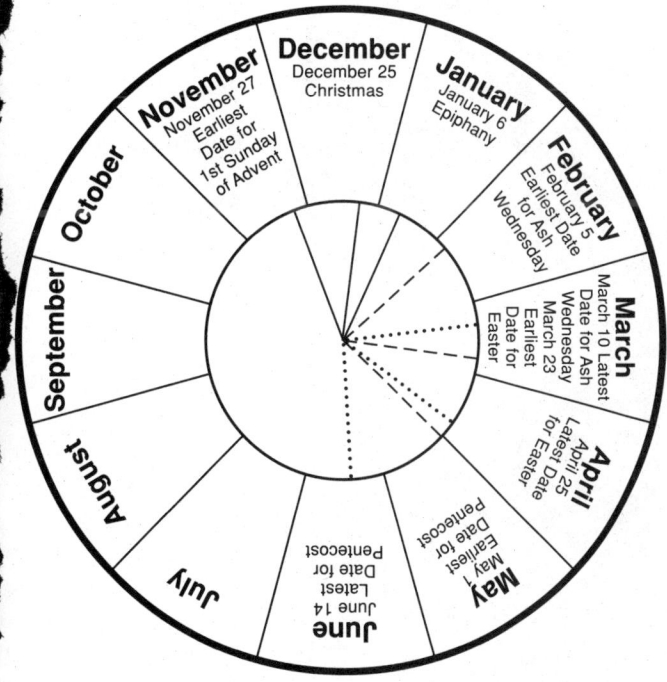

Ordinary time is the period between Epiphany and Ash Wednesday and between Pentecost and the First Sunday of Advent

Key:
- - - - -   Lent may occur during this period
_____   Denotes periods of Advent and Christmas
....   Denotes the period of Easter to Pentecost

STRESS & TIME

GROUP INTERACTION

Together design a stress-buster event to celebrate the joy of a group member. Or celebrate something good that happened to your group. Ask:

★ *Would you include ritual, music, special clothing?*

Be sure your event meets the standards for a real celebration. Is it enriching? creative? energizing? fun?

DISCUSSION

Invite group members to record rituals they associate with each of the celebrations listed. Ask:

★ *Which are religious? patriotic? secular? combinations?*

★ *Is any special music connected with each ritual? special clothing? special foods? worship?*

GROUP INTERACTION

Ahead of time, provide two baskets, each with different colored "time bits." "Time bits" can be small squares of two different colors of construction paper, or dried beans and corn. At least sixteen "time bits" will be needed per person. Each "time bit" represents one hour of time. Label one basket "Input Time." The second basket should be labeled "Output Time." Input time energizes people, while output time uses up energy. Sabbath time (rest) and celebrations are both considered input time.

REJOICE WITH OTHERS

In Christian community, when one member weeps, we all feel sad, if one is honored we rejoice together (1 Corinthians 12:26). Many holidays and parties are celebrations over the good fortune of a friend.

Modern Rituals

Event	Ritual
Fourth of July	fireworks, parade, picnic
Marriage	wedding ceremony, reception, honeymoon
Homecoming	Football game, queen, dance
Confirmation	
Spring break	
Graduation	
Communion	
Relocation	
Senior Year	
Birthday	
New Year	
Family vacation	

DOES TIME ENERGIZE?

Depending on our personalities, some of us need more time than others to be renewed. For example, introverts find that spending a great deal of time talking with others drains them of energy. They need to get away from others in order to renew their energy and their spirits. On the other hand, extroverts find themselves being renewed by people and people related activities. An introvert is drained by a few hours of partying with friends. Extroverts feel great after attending a party—and often are rarin' to go to yet another!

YOUTHSEARCH

Ask group members to choose one day during the past week and list awake hours and activities. On each line each member lays down hour bits from a particular basket to indicate whether time was input or output.

Say: "Remember you may regard an activity as input while another person lists it as output."

Input and output time need not be identically balanced; the balance should fit with the rhythm of a person's life.

Ask:

★ Is your time out-of-synch or running smoothly?

★ What changes would you like to make?

★ How might you do this?

★ If the balance were better, would your stress be reduced?

★ Assign partners from among the total group. Partners should explain their individual days to each other.

Everyone requires rest and renewal, whether extroverted or introverted. How we become renewed differs, but we all need renewal in order to continue to be healthy.

Sabbath rest and celebrations are simply two different ways to accomplish an important purpose!

Day_____

HOUR	ACTIVITY	TIME BIT

STRESS & TIME

DISCUSSION

Ask:

★ Are your meals in school times of stress or shalom? your family meals? church potlucks?

★ Describe a meal which for you symbolized a bond of friendship.

WORSHIP

Invite your pastor to celebrate the Sacrament of Holy Communion with your group.
OR
Place a pitcher of iced water, surrounded by small paper cups on a tray, in the center of your group.

Read Isaiah 55:1-3a.

Say: "This water symbolizes the abundant life from God that is free to us. We are invited to drink of this water."

Offer a cup of cold water to each group member to drink. Close with a simple prayer, thanking God for providing true food and water for an abundant life.

EATING AND DRINKING TOGETHER

What goes on at every celebration? Eating does, of course! No party is complete without good food. Food symbolizes the bond of friendship. Yet in our culture we often sit down with strangers in a fast food restaurant and "eat on the run".

Not so in biblical times. To invite a person to a meal in one's home showed honor. It was an offer of peace, trust, mutuality, and forgiveness. In short, sharing a table meant sharing life. Refusal to break bread was a mark of anger and a symbol of a rupture in friendship. In Judaism, table fellowship meant communion together before God, so the meal took on religious as well as social significance. Thus Jesus' practice of eating and drinking with the poor and unclean expressed his mission and anticipated the heavenly banquet in the end time.

Our Lord said to his disciples: "You are those who have stood by me in my trials; and I confer on you, just as my Father has conferred on me, a kingdom, so that you may eat and drink at my table in my kingdom." (Luke 22:28-30) The celebration in heaven will be like a wedding banquet and all are invited (See the parable of the Wedding Banquet, Matthew 22:1-14). All our earthly celebrations will be as nothing in comparison.

At the Last Supper, before his death, Jesus used the Passover symbols of bread and wine to signify his body broken in death. Jesus gave himself as food and drink for his dear friends. It is the death and resurrection of Jesus that we celebrate every time we share in Holy Communion. That symbolic banquet anticipates the time we will eat together as community at a banquet in heaven. Then we will be more closely united with God than food and drink are with our bodies.

YOUTHSEARCH

AN INVITATION TO ABUNDANT LIFE

> Ho, everyone who thirsts,
>   come to the waters;
> and you that have no money,
>   come, buy and eat!
> Come, buy wine and milk
>   without money and without
>   price.
> Why do you spend your money
>   for that which is not bread,
> and your labor for that which
>   does not satisfy?
> Listen carefully to me, and eat
>   what is good,
> and delight yourself in rich
>   food.
> Incline your ear, and come to
>   me;
>   listen, so that you may live.
>   (Isaiah 55:1-3a)

READ THE OLD TESTAMENT BOOK OF ECCLESIASTES.

If you are unable to read the entire Old Testament book of Ecclesiastes, read a short portion of it. Ecclesiastes 3 reminds us that life is designed in balance. There are times for laughter but also for tears, peace and war, planting and harvesting. There are seasons for renewal and for hectic activity. Balance, however, is essential!

FOR NEXT TIME

Ask group members to read as much as possible of the book of Ecclesiastes before the next session. At the very least have them read Ecclesiastes 3.

If your group enjoys creative outlets, encourage group members to bring an item, such as a symbol, or a drawing, that expresses the meaning of Ecclesiastes 3. Share these expressions as you begin the next session.

STRESS & TIME

JOURNAL PAGE

CHAPTER 6

The Present Time

GROUP ENERGIZER

Invite group members to draw "My Own Time Line," on newsprint. Have group members draw a line, symbolizing their lives, from left to right. Divide the line into three sections: "Past," "Present," and "Future."

In the section labeled "Past," each individual should record major events—good or bad—that have influenced who they are now. Do the same with names of influential people. When all have finished, instruct group members to pair up with a partner and discuss their chart.

RETHINKING TIME

So far we have visualized time as ordinary and holy. Sabbath and holidays are included in holy time. Everything else is ordinary time. Conceiving time as being either ordinary or holy is not the only way to think about time. Another way is to consider time as being past, present, or future oriented.

How would you explain our divisions of time into past, present, and future? How are both past and future contained in the present? How are they separate? Do you believe love transcends time and continues beyond death? How might that affect the way we spend time now?

Our way of conceiving time as past/present/future is not the only way. One of the most ancient and creative Christian traditions, the Celtic church, which existed from the fifth to the twelfth centuries in northern England and Ireland, believed time was a sacred reality blessed and already redeemed by God's compassion. For them the present contained within itself both past events, which continue to live on, as well as the seeds of future events waiting to be born. There was no clear mark between past, present and future. They told legends in which contemporary saints helped as midwives to Mary, the mother of Jesus. Relationships transcended time and people of similar qualities, no matter when the people lived on earth, existed together as friends. They believed in "thin places," geographical locations where one could momentarily encounter a more ancient reality within the present, or in a glance be transported into the future. Their beliefs affirmed that death could never destroy bonds of love.

STRESS & TIME

REFLECTION

Invite youth to reflect again on their time lines, developed earlier in the session. Instruct youth to note the word "Past" on their time line. Ask them to list any fears that they are dragging along from the past.

Read aloud the suggestions for letting go of the past (see "Fears from the Past").

Ask:

★ *Which suggestions apply to your situation?*

★ *What is a first step you might take to let go of a fear from the past?*

FEARS FROM THE PAST

A contemporary psychologist suggests that most of our stress comes from dragging along fears from a past time or projecting anxieties into future time. We become burdened by fears from the past or anxieties about the future. We rarely live in the present moment. If we stop and look at the present moment NOW–it's usually good. In this view of time, everything happens in the present moment, for NOW we remember the past and imagine the future. The past and future exist only in our minds. It is always really NOW.

Hanging on to a painful past can cause present fear, anxiety, stress, and loss of energy. We may be dragging a sack full of stuff such as separation pain due to the divorce of parents; death of a beloved person or pet; guilt (real or unjustified); experiences of violence, abuse, incest, unfaithfulness of a friend, unloving parents, alcoholism of a family member. These wounds may be deep and powerful. The pain acts as a shadow and continues to hover and cloud our present. Sometimes fears are repressed and we may need professional help to even identify them.

Until we let go of the fears retained from times in the past, they will continue causing stress in the present. It is not easy, and healing may take a long time, but there is a path out.

- **Acknowledge that the old story is over.** Stop asking why. Stop blaming yourself. There are no adequate reasons. It was and now is no more. Cut your ties with the old story.

- **Admit honest feelings.** "I was hurt because my mother never had time for me." It may take a long time for fear and anger to run its course. That's OK. You have every right to honest feelings and no reason to feel guilty for them.

- **Stop running away from pain.** Gently let the pain "break your heart." Cry as often as it feels good, for it will bring comfort. Continue to walk, one step at a time, through pain to joy.

- **Forgive.** You are not forgiving the hurtful act for that will never be right. You are forgiving the actors who behaved out of their own pain and confusion, lack of skill, and humanity. You need to forgive, not

DISCUSSION

Return, once again, to the time lines developed earlier in the session. Call attention to the section marked "Future." Invite youth to list anxieties they project about the future. For example, one youth doing this activity noted such fears as "I'm afraid I won't get into my first choice college" and "Will there be a job for me when I graduate from college?"

Invite group members to share some of their anxieties if they are willing. Record anxieties from willing participants on a chalkboard or a large sheet of paper. Ask:

★ *Which seem like real possibilities and which seem imagined?*

★ *How might you better prepare for and control future events?*

★ *What do Jesus' words teach about priorities?*

★ *Would different priorities reduce stress? Explain.*

★ *If you followed Jesus' teachings do you believe your future would "fall into place?"*

---

because the actors deserve to be forgiven, but because you deserve to break free. If we hold on to the hurts of the past, we are trapped in a cycle with those persons forever. The only way to overcome evil is with good (Romans 12:20). God loves and forgives us, no matter what we do, and gratitude for our own forgiveness can save us from the fearful clutches of evil done to us.

If your fears from the past are repressed or extremely painful, seek help from a counselor, a pastor, or a trusted adult friend.

ANXIETY ABOUT THE FUTURE

Most of us are handling the present just fine, but we may fear some unforseen future time. We experience stress because we might not get invited to the prom, receive good grades, get accepted into college, find a good job, or be happily married. We worry that at some future time we will be given more than we can handle, not measure up, sink under great pain, or look like a fool. We may feel terrified that time might bring more than we can bear.

When we anticipate the worst, a cloud from the future hangs back over the present. Yet much of the anxiety projected into the future exists primarily in our minds. The present is real, and most fears of the future turn out not as badly as anticipated or never even occur at all.

Jesus said, "Therefore I tell you, do not worry about your life, what you will eat or what you will drink, or about your body, what you will wear . . . But strive first for the kingdom of God and his righteousness, and all these things will be given to you as well." (Matthew 6:25,33)

STRESS & TIME

DECISION POINT

If time is short or if you are exploring this chapter over more than one session, break here. End your time together with prayer, assigning prayer partners from within the group.

PULSE POINT

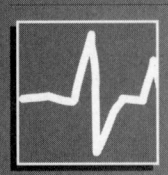

Think about the New Testament's use of three words to describe time.

Ask:

★ *Can you recall a recent kairos moment? a recent chronos moment? an aion?*

BIBLE STUDY

Read Ecclesiastes 3:1-9 aloud. Invite the group to look at their own present.

Ask:

★ *What are some "timely" activities for you now?*

★ *What activities might be "out of synch" with your age, emotional maturity, education, income, or gender?*

BIBLE STUDY

Have the group read Ecclesiastes 3:9-15.

Ask:

★ *What part of you do you believe will live on after your time on earth ends? (Ecclesiastes 5:14-16)*

★ *How might that affect the way you use your time now?*

★ *Do you believe eating, drinking and enjoying work is a gift from God? Explain.*

IS IT ALL GREEK TO YOU?

In the New Testament, three words are used to reflect different "feelings" of time. Each of them is a Greek word:

• **chronos** is often used to describe a "quantity" of time. Read John 7:33 to get a "feel" for chronos.

• **kairos** is usually used to describe a "quality" of time and is used in Mark 1:15 and John 7:8.

• **aion** is used to describe a "broad sweep" of time. We get our word *eon* from *aion*.

Whichever word is used, the New Testament proclaims that God is the one who transcends time, remaining faithful and constant.

GOD TRANSCENDS TIME

The religious view in latter Old Testament times is that bad people suffer and good people prosper. God wills it that way and God's justice sees to it that things happened that way. The book of Proverbs represents this philosophy. However, in the book of Job (Chapter 2) we see a challenge to the theory in the story of a rich, happy, righteous man whose fortune turned and who then suffered immensely. The easy formula breaks down and Job challenges God to provide answers. However, the writer of Ecclesiastes looks at life and decides there simply are no answers. We cannot know details of how, when and why. All appears as vanity, futility, chasing after the wind (Ecclesiastes 1:1-11). Many think this gives his writing a dark, cynical, depressive ring. But on the other hand, his profound experience of the vanity and fleetingness of life, evident in the inability of humans to control time, leads him to an even more profound experience of God. **God is the one who transcends time and who remains consistent and faithful.**

Just as we can observe the seasons moving forward with regularity so the times of a human life are locked into a pattern. There exists a rhythm and each event has its own appointed time. If we are tuned in to this rhythm, appropriate activities can be chosen for various times. What is right at one time may lead to disaster at another. Timing is important. Each verse in Ecclesiastes contains two opposite pairs, which are in most cases somehow related to each other. The poem represents the heights and depths of a human life. This is how the writer observed time.

The writer's reflections then follow. He posed the same question (Ecclesiastes 1:9) as in 1:2-11 about what people gain from all their toil. The answer is nothing! It simply passes away as the next generation appears. Our gains do not outlast death. God gave humans a sense of past and future, yet kept from us complete knowledge of what happened before or will happen after our lifetimes (1:11).

EMBRACE THE PRESENT

Therefore, since we cannot know the past or the future, the best we can do is enjoy the present. At the very point when he gave up figuring everything out, when he let go of control of all things, the writer of Ecclesiastes found truth. God simply wanted humans to be happy and enjoy themselves as long as they live, to eat, drink, and take pleasure in their toil. This is a gift from God (Ecclesiastes 1:13). (Note that the writer believes in following God and God's commandments [12:13]. Enjoying life does not mean "doing anything you feel like doing.")

The biblical writer radiated a sense of security within the insecurity of time because God acts consistently—forever. To this nothing can be added or taken away. All who see this are in awe of God (12:14). The writer understood time as anchored in eternity and this gave him unshakable trust in God and nothing more is necessary. God is dependable!

The writer broke free of a stressful life of striving, profits, gain, and worry. All he saw was vanity and futility. Instead he exhibited a remarkable freedom to embrace the present NOW and enjoy the ordinary pleasures of sweetness of sunlight (Ecclesiastes 11:7), food, drink, and work (4:13); comfort and dressing up (9:8); youth (11:9); friendship (4:9-12); and the "woman he loves" (9:9). He found joy in simple things because they are God's gifts.

REFLECTION

Invite group members to refer to the "Now" section of the their time lines. Encourage them to let go of fears from the past and anxieties about the future. Say: "Using the space provided on pages 50-53, write about this present chapter of your life."

STRESS & TIME

CONSIDER THE PRESENT TIME

• Name the people or activities that are important to you at this time:

• What are your physical qualities? health?

• What feelings predominate your life?

• Evaluate this chapter of this volume of YOUTH-SEARCH by giving it a grade. (A, B, C, or D)

• Would you give your life (today) a letter grade of an A, B, C, or D? Explain.

YOUTHSEARCH

WORSHIP

Read the text aloud. On a large sheet of paper or chalkboard, list joys suggested by the group. Read the list of joys as a litany. After the group reads the list, ask the group to respond with the phrase, "Thank you, Gracious God, for the gift of time."

A GIFT FROM GOD

My conclusion is this:
true happiness lies in eating and drinking and enjoying
whatever has been achieved under the sun, throughout the life given by God: for this is the lot of humanity. And whenever God gives someone riches and property, with the ability to enjoy them and to find contentment in work, this is a gift from God. For such a person will hardly notice the passing of time, so long as God keeps his heart occupied with joy.
(Ecclesiastes 5:17-19, New Jerusalem Bible)

STRESS & TIME

GROUP INTERACTION

Build and fly kites together! To build a kite:

1. Lay a thirty inch stick across a thirty-six inch stick, eight inches down from the top.

2. Tie the two sticks tightly together with kite string or twine.

3. Cut notches in the ends of the sticks with a sharp knife.

4. Run string through the notches and around the outside edges of the kite, winding it around each end a few times.

5. Lay the kite frame on a piece of wrapping or butcher paper.

6. Cut the paper two inches larger than the frame. Glue.

7. Color or mark as desired.

Enjoy the freedom of celebration! Schedule a time to fly your kites as a group. For fun, you might want to put a letter on the back of each kite to spell YouthSearch. Can you get the kites synchronized so that you can actually read YouthSearch? Take a photograph!

CELEBRATE THE PRESENT

For years now, the Indian Christians of Guatemala have faced poverty and persecution from their government. But each November these Christians celebrate All Saints' Day or the Day of the Dead. On that day, the whole community gathers to eat, socialize, and fly kites. Some of the kites are huge octagonal kites, brightly colored in reds and blues. Other kites, small and round, are attached by string to children's hands. Each November, all the kites catch the wind and fly skyward, dancing and leaping for all to see.

The Christians of Guatemala build kites and watch them fly, even in the face of hunger, persecution, and death. Even when the present moment remains clouded, they celebrate because time is a gift from God.

As our study ends, go in joy! May God's *shalom* remain with you!

Journal Page

The YouthSearch Group Experience

Your YouthSearch group will be unique. The youth who participate will contribute their own perspectives, feelings, experiences, yearnings. They will work and learn together in distinctive ways.

As we developed YOUTHSEARCH, we imagined youth and adults exploring a crucial area of daily life and discovering a spirituality that would strengthen their decisions and actions. Every volume of YOUTHSEARCH focuses on a specific concern that can be explored in six or more sessions. It is designed for small groups and for time periods of ninety minutes. The book can be used in a variety of settings. Although it was not planned for use in Sunday school, you may choose to adapt it for the length of time available on Sunday morning. "Bringing YOUTHSEARCH to Sunday Morning," on page 55, will help you adapt the material for your group.

A YouthSearch group is composed of youth and an adult leader. They come together to learn about a particular issue and to grow in Christian faith and discipleship. Your group will meet on a regular basis. The sessions will be informal; they will not feel like schoolwork. Creating an atmosphere of honesty, openness, and trust will allow the youth to struggle with their own spiritual development. In fact, a YouthSearch group may become a miniature community of faith as the members of the group support and encourage one another, emphasize their relationship with Christ, and become more aware of each person's spiritual development.

Many YouthSearch groups create and adhere to a covenant that specifies the purposes, the hopes, and the expectations of the group. If the participants in your group decide to create a covenant, be sure they review it often so that it continues to call them toward a common faith and life.

Bringing YouthSearch to Sunday Morning

Although YouthSearch was not created specifically for Sunday school, it can be adapted so that it provides a terrific resource for small groups of youth who meet on Sunday morning. If you decide to use YouthSearch on Sunday morning, be creative and flexible in adapting it for your group.

The most significant change you make will be to adjust sessions so that they fit the time avaliable to your group. YouthSearch is designed for ninety-minute sessions, but you may have only thirty or forty-five minutes. Pay careful attention to the Decision Point icons. They will suggest an appropriate place to divide each chapter into more than one session. Use the Decision Point to help you divide the chapter into shorter sessions that will work for your group on Sunday morning.

When adapting YouthSearch for your group, keep in mind the basic parts of each session. Every time your group meets you will probably want to include an opening activity that will help the youth feel at ease, Bible study, discussion, time for reflection that will encourage the youth to apply what they have learned to their lives, a closing activity, and a time to look ahead to the next session.

By using the icons and planning carefully, you can use YouthSearch to open the door for lively, stimulating discussions about issues that are crucial for the youth in your group.

Using YouthSearch on Sunday morning will provide opportunities for the youth to help lead sessions. Group members will develop a sense of community when they practice openness, hospitality, and candor during YouthSearch meetings. Participants may not attend every Sunday; so during every session, emphasize the need to call people who were absent and to encourage their participation.

YouthSearch groups offer participants an environment in which to explore critical life issues, to experience the life-giving Christian community, and to develop skills that are crucial for their faith. Thoughtful planning will create an atmosphere of friendliness and mutuality that can turn Sunday morning groups into communities of caring and learning.

STRESS & TIME

Starting a YouthSearch Group

All you need to start a YouthSearch group is interest and investment. Youth are more likely to get excited about topics that relate to areas of their lives that are of interest and concern to them. Selection of a topic and careful preparation will show the members of your group that you are interested in them.

Preparation is crucial. YOUTHSEARCH is designed to be used with small groups of people who have come together to learn and to grow in faith.

To start a YouthSearch group,

▶ begin by reading *Start Up!: Preparing to Lead Your Small Group*, the first volume in the YOUTHSEARCH series. *Start Up!* offers practical suggestions for leading a small group. It will help you develop your skills and build your confidence.

▶ begin with one of the books in the YOUTHSEARCH series. Read the articles, such as this one, that appear in the back of the book.

What's the right size for a YouthSearch group? The ideal size of a small group is between four and twelve people. If more than twelve youth are interested in participating, invite them to form more than one group. If they prefer to stay in one group, be aware that some youth may feel uncomfortable talking openly in a large group. Plan sessions that include activities for smaller groups.

In many churches, small groups provide the setting for study, fellowship, mission, and worship.

All you need to start a YouthSearch group is interest and investment.

Small groups are formed to encourage interaction, to prepare people for membership, to include new members in the life of the church, to explore difficult life issues.

Work with the participants to make decisions that will affect the size or the personality of the group. Ask them to consider issues such as creating a new group, inviting new members to join the group, or changing its purpose.

Youth respond to personal invitations. Follow up invitations with phone calls or notes to confirm their participation. When you invite youth to participate, be sure to tell them the topic, the names of other group members, and meeting times and places.

Emphasize the importance of attending each meeting of the small group. Unavoidable emergencies may occur. Make note of absences; call group members who miss a session and let them know they were missed.

Before you start a YouthSearch group, be sure you know the answers to these questions:

▶ Who's going to lead the group or groups?

Will you be leading all the sessions? Will you and another leader be present at every session? Will you recruit leaders who will learn to lead their own groups by working first with you or another experienced leader?

▶ Where will your group meet?

Meeting at the church has advantages and disadvantages. Would your group prefer to meet in someone's home? If you meet away from the church, what arrangements for transportation will you make? If you decide to meet in a person's home, how will you ensure that interruptions and distractions are kept to a minimum?

▶ How will you get everyone a copy of YOUTHSEARCH before the first meeting?

The members of the group may want to look over the book before they meet. During the first meeting, invite the participants to become familiar with the book's topic, purpose, and contents.

▶ Will your group be open to new members or will other people wait for a new group to be formed?

We suggest that you encourage the youth to join the group during the first or the second session. If other youth want to be part of the group after the second session, ask them to wait until another group is formed.

Your group may work through only one book in the YOUTHSEARCH series. Or you may design your educational program around the topics in YOUTHSEARCH. First impressions are important. Be sure to prepare carefully for the first sessions with your new YouthSearch group.

STRESS & TIME

Tips for Lively Discussions

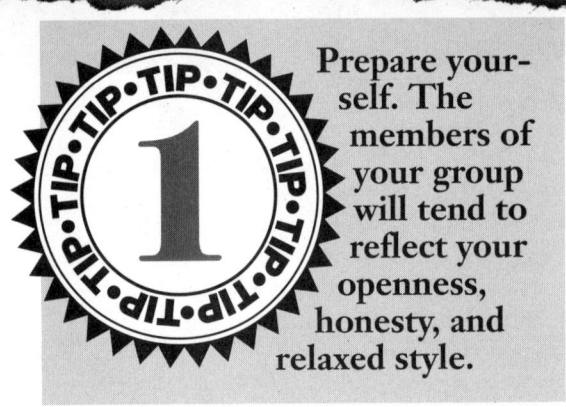

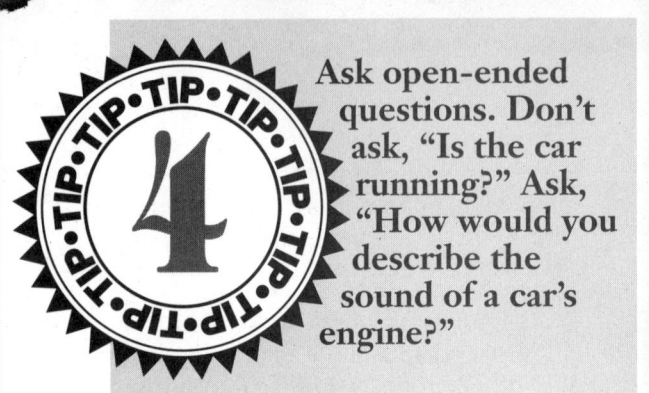

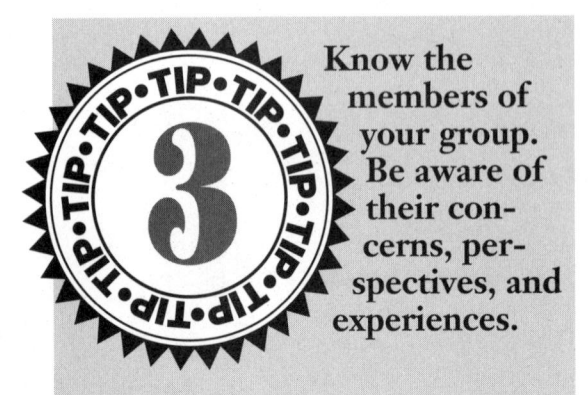

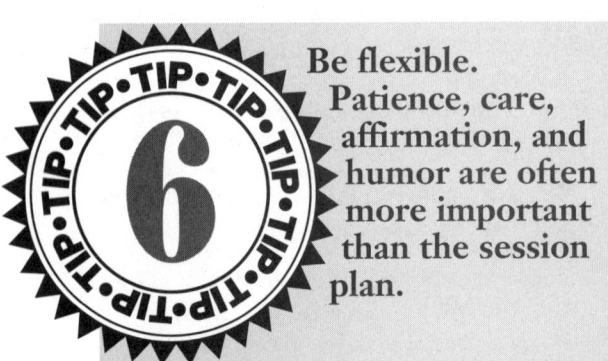

TIP 1 — Prepare yourself. The members of your group will tend to reflect your openness, honesty, and relaxed style.

TIP 2 — Don't lecture. Your job is to lead a discussion, not to convey information or to cover a prescribed section of the material.

TIP 3 — Know the members of your group. Be aware of their concerns, perspectives, and experiences.

TIP 4 — Ask open-ended questions. Don't ask, "Is the car running?" Ask, "How would you describe the sound of a car's engine?"

TIP 5 — Ask follow-up questions. If someone in the group makes an interesting statement or offers a unique perspective, ask, "Why do you say that?" or say, "Tell us more about that."

TIP 6 — Be flexible. Patience, care, affirmation, and humor are often more important than the session plan.

YOUTHSEARCH

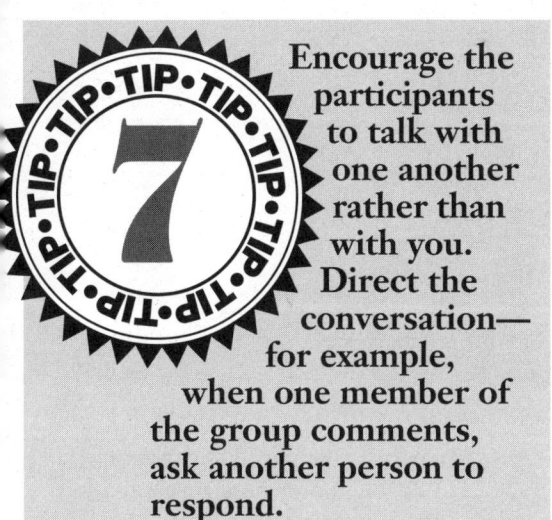

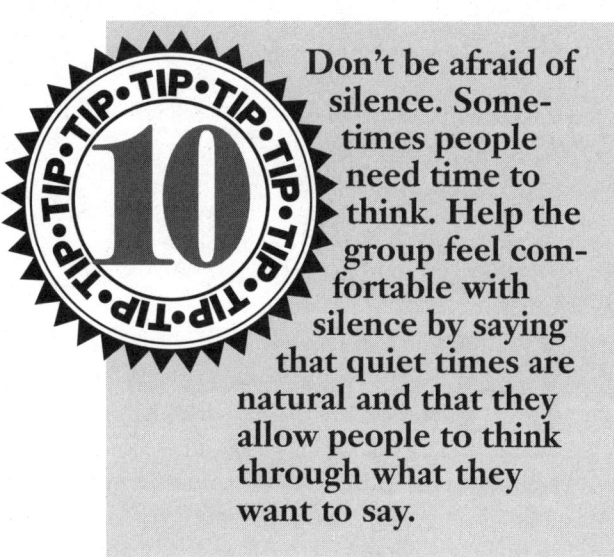

TIP 7 Encourage the participants to talk with one another rather than with you. Direct the conversation—for example, when one member of the group comments, ask another person to respond.

TIP 8 Trust your group. Let the group lead discussions. Let the group set the agenda. Your task is to serve the group and to facilitate the group's discussion.

TIP 9 Monitor the conversation. Don't try to do everything. Use the options offered in YOUTHSEARCH to create a balance between taking on too much of the topic and doing too little.

TIP 10 Don't be afraid of silence. Sometimes people need time to think. Help the group feel comfortable with silence by saying that quiet times are natural and that they allow people to think through what they want to say.

TIP 11 At any time, an individual may choose not to participate in the discussion. People who need time to think about a response or who choose not to comment should be able to say, "pass," without feeling uncomfortable.

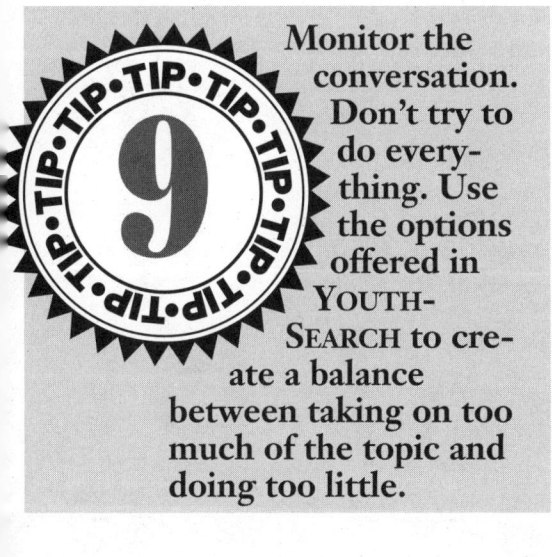

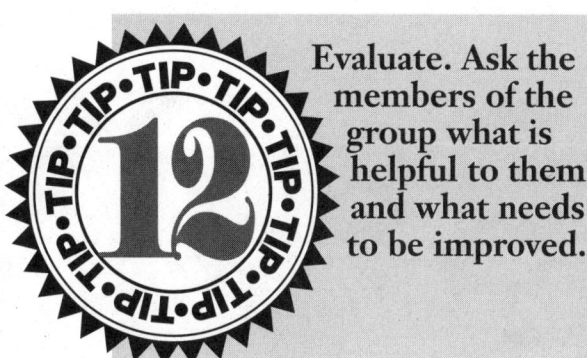

TIP 12 Evaluate. Ask the members of the group what is helpful to them and what needs to be improved.

STRESS & TIME

Taking Your Group's Pulse

How can you tell if your Youth-Search group is healthy? We determine if a person is healthy by taking his or her pulse and listening to his or her heart. Evaluating the vitality of a group is perhaps more subtle, but there are ways to determine the health of your group and ways to strengthen its heartbeat.

Check the group's pulse at the beginning of each session. Pulse Point icons identify times to assess the group's feelings. At the end of each session, encourage the participants to complete the chart on page 61. Then begin the next session by asking volunteers to report their responses. If you have more than six sessions, photocopy page 61; and give each participant a copy.

▶ Keep the group aware of its covenant.

At the beginning of each session, invite the participants to recall the commitment they have made to the group. During your review of the covenant, you may detect waning or shifting interest. At this point, members of the group may choose to change the covenant so that it more clearly reflects their concerns and expectations.

▶ Pay attention to the atmosphere of the group.

Jesus created an atmosphere in which the disciples knew that they would be accepted and loved even when they failed. When discussing tough issues, some members of your group may wonder if they will be accepted if their positions are different from those of other people in the group. Be aware of discomfort, hesitation, or uncertainty.

▶ Keep an eye on absences or tardiness.

If a group member is repeatedly late or absent, he or she may feel uncomfortable with what's happening in the group. Regular absence and tardiness hurts the group. Respond immediately; talk to the person; find out what's happening.

▶ Unpack a session or two with a person or two.

Immediately following a group meeting, ask one or two participants to talk with you about the session. Ask: What was exciting? boring? interesting? Listen to what they say; and in the next session, make changes that reflect their concerns.

YouthSearch Pulse Record

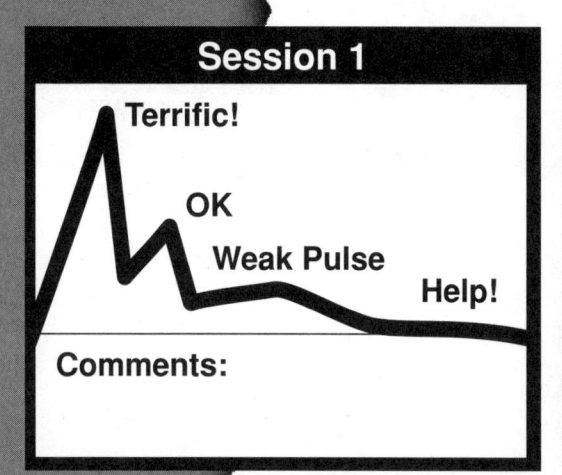

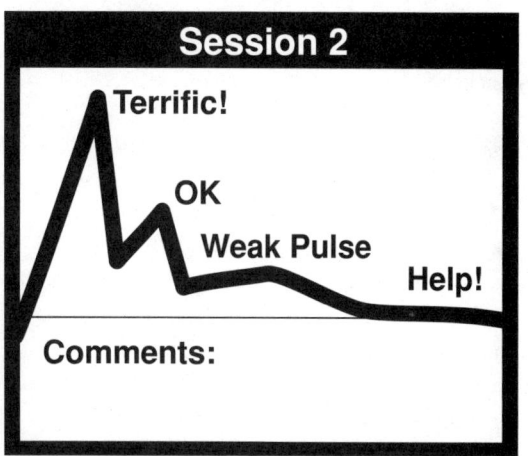

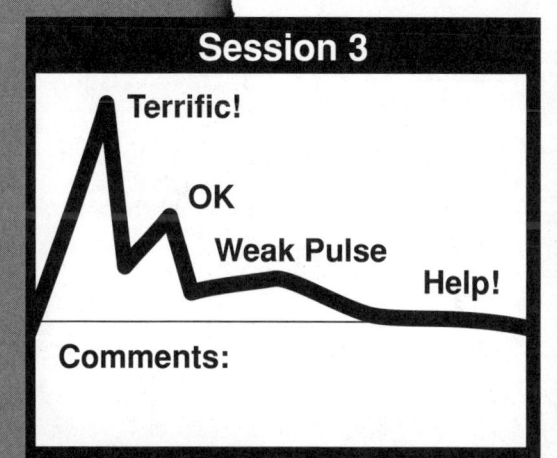

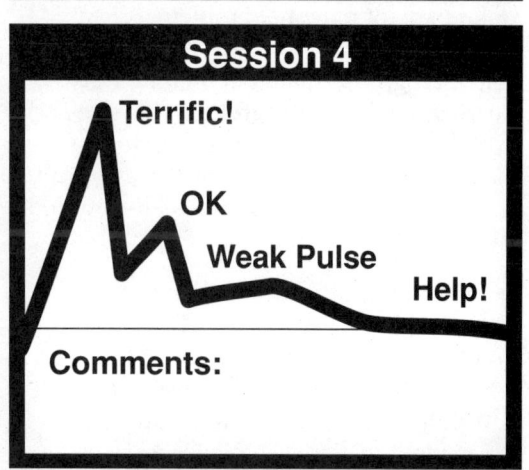

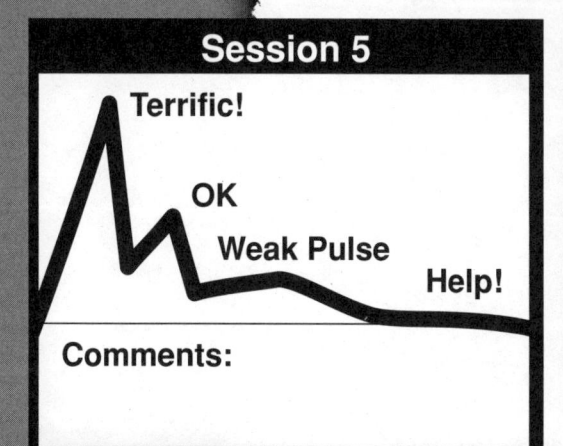

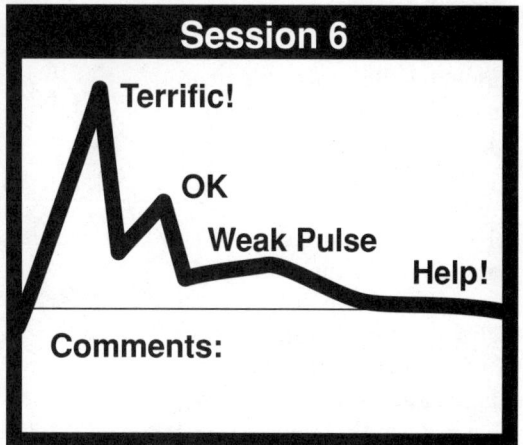

Session 1
Terrific!
OK
Weak Pulse
Help!
Comments:

Session 2
Terrific!
OK
Weak Pulse
Help!
Comments:

Session 3
Terrific!
OK
Weak Pulse
Help!
Comments:

Session 4
Terrific!
OK
Weak Pulse
Help!
Comments:

Session 5
Terrific!
OK
Weak Pulse
Help!
Comments:

Session 6
Terrific!
OK
Weak Pulse
Help!
Comments:

• YouthSearch © 1995 by Abingdon Press. Permission is granted to reproduce this page for use with your YouthSearch group. •

STRESS & TIME

Dealing With Group Problems

People bring energy and excitement to a group. They also bring their own ideas and their own unique ways of struggling with issues. Everyone is creative, but creativity comes in different shapes and sizes. So the group may face conflict and disagreement. How can you most effectively deal with group problems?

▶ Prepare for potential problems. Great small groups don't just happen. Leaders help their groups maintain their identity by clearly articulating the group's purpose and by helping members of the group to stay focused on the topic. Leaders also create an atmosphere in which questions are honored and learning is valued.

▶ Practice the attitudes and skills that you want the group to learn. Small groups don't just discuss information. The group leader teaches by example the attitudes and skills needed for small group interaction: tolerance, patience, caring, and support.

▶ Remember that conflict is inevitable. Becoming a mature group is impossible without conflict. The participants in a YouthSearch group care about the topic and will express strong feelings and opinions. As the leader of the group, you can help participants identify the sources of conflict and facilitate further discussion. You may also suggest that the group members agree to disagree. Remind the youth that being members of a group means supporting and respecting one another even when they disagree.

▶ Remember that problems may be the result of diversity in the group and the growing pains of adolescence. Be sure to listen to everyone's opinion, to recognize differences, and to accept each person as a unique individual. Consider: The problem may not be the more obvious sources of conflict, but the relationships among the group members. In the disciples' relationship with Jesus, they became servants of God in their daily ministry of compassion. The relationships among the people in your YouthSearch group should help them to grow in faith and service.

Our YouthSearch Group

Name	Address	Phone Number

Notes